## WAS THERE A PLACE CALLED ATLANTIS?

Long before my involvement in "Star Trek" I was a voyager in the special world that seems to exist just beyond our own perceptions. And so I was intrigued by Alan Landsburg's invitation to narrate the first film in his new TV series.

When I saw the pilot film my anticipations were confirmed. The images stayed with me long after the viewing. I was tantalized by the vision of Easter Island's giant, sightless monoliths; the crumbling, uneven lines of an Egyptian step pyramid; the blue-black cliffs of volcanic ash that buried the isle of Thera. What caught my fancy was the way in which the film was put together to unravel a mystery that has bedeviled archaeologists for centuries. Was there a place called Atlantis?

Not only does Alan venture into lost civilizations, but in time he investigates extraterrestrials, strange phenomena, myths and monsters, magic and witchcraft and missing persons whose disappearances are inexplicable.

The prospects are exciting . . . We're promised an immense amount of pleasure. Each program, each book, will be a deep immersion in an important quest. Please join us.

LEONARD NIMOY

Bantam Books by Alan Landsburg
Ask your bookseller for the books you have missed

IN SEARCH OF ANCIENT MYSTERIES
(with Sally Landsburg)
IN SEARCH OF LOST CIVILIZATIONS
THE OUTER SPACE CONNECTION
(with Sally Landsburg)

# IN SEARCH OF LOST CIVILIZATIONS

Alan Landsburg

IN SEARCH OF LOST CIVILIZATIONS
*A Bantam Book / December 1976*

Insert photographs from South America by *Deborah Blum;* photos from Europe and the Near East by *Andrew Reichline;* photos from Peru by *Tony Halik.*



ISBN 0-553-10582-5

*Published simultaneously in the United States and Canada*

---

*Bantam Books are published by Bantam Books, Inc. Its trademark, consisting of the words "Bantam Books" and the portrayal of a bantam, is registered in the United States Patent Office and in other countries. Marca Registrada. Bantam Books, Inc., 666 Fifth Avenue, New York, New York 10019.*

---

PRINTED IN THE UNITED STATES OF AMERICA

To MARVIN KOSLOW
whose energy and determination
made "In Search Of . . ." a reality
and whose friendship has added a warming
luster to my life

and to LINDA
whose love and support
broaden my vistas beyond
the boundaries of the farthest horizon

## ACKNOWLEDGMENT

My editorial associate in this book
was KEITH MONROE. His *own* fascination
with the classical outlines of history
has infused this book with a special luster.

## AUTHOR'S NOTE

The chronicle of discovery amassed in this volume is the work of many people. More than 100 researchers, scientists and skilled filmmakers participated in the various quests. For simplicity's sake we have comingled our experiences into a single first person narrative so that we may share with you the essence and excitement of the hunt without a clutter of personal introductions. As author and chief chronicler of the work we have done, I owe an enormous debt of gratitude to those who joined me in the field to explore the world of mystery. To all of those dedicated workers committed to "In Search Of . . ." I say thank you. This book is as much yours as mine.

*Alan Landsburg*

# CONTENTS

## FOREWORD

The images stayed with me long after I had finished viewing the film. I was tantalized by the vision of Easter Island's giant, sightless monoliths, the crumbling, uneven lines of an Egyptian step pyramid, the blue-black cliffs of volcanic ash that buried the isle of Thera. Each of the sites was sufficiently intriguing in itself. What caught my fancy was the manner in which they had been organized in order to unravel a mystery that has bedeviled archeologists for centuries. Was there a place called Atlantis?

The film was the pilot effort in a television series that Alan Landsburg had been commissioned to produce. He had asked me to look at the film in order to narrate the story told in the production. As the lights came up in the screening room, I was certain of two facts. First, a hundred questions about Atlantis, the civilization of ancient Egypt, the chronicles of Sumerian digs were crackling around in my mind. Secondly, I was hooked. It was, in many respects, a dream assignment. Before me was an opportunity to explore the great mysteries of the past and present with Alan, a highly credible documentary filmmaker with an impressive roll call of credits that included the "National Geographic Specials" and "The Undersea World of Jacques Cousteau." The new series, Alan promised, would reach as far out as possible in an effort to shed new light on subjects that baffle modern scientists. The occult, psychic perception, radical archeology were all to be part of the fabric of the series. It was like a homecoming for me. Long before my involvement in "Star Trek," I was a voyager in the special world that seems to exist just beyond our own perceptions.

The list of subjects was perfect. Not only would we

venture into lost civilizations like Atlantis, but in time we would investigate extraterrestrials, strange phenomena, myths and monsters, magic and witchcraft and missing persons whose disappearances are inexplicable.

I knew I would have an immense amount of pure pleasure in being associated with the film series. Each week has been a deep immersion in an exciting quest. In this book Alan has chronicled the routes he's followed "In Seach Of . . ."—the rare and wonderful tales that are hidden in the dim outlines of ancient worlds and almost imperceptible events. The hunt was a wonderful experience for us, and I think you'll find it equally delightful in the re-telling.

*Leonard Nimoy*

## PROLOGUE

The green leafed dome of the Peruvian rain forest shut out fresh air and wetness pervaded our senses. The click, whirl and hum of insects made us feel we were inside a gigantic loudspeaker broadcasting static interference. The physical effort of hacking through jungle enervated us. At times it was hard to recollect why we were here at all. The drudgery of the march replaced the bubbling optimism of the expedition's start.

We were seeking an X on a map, an X that we had reason to believe was the last undiscovered citadel of the ancient Incan empire. The damp heat of the trek had sapped our enthusiasm. We were making slow headway, some four to six miles a day.

The clang of a machete hitting rock snapped us out of lethargy. In the wake of the sound came a shout of pure exaltation. We had literally walked into a wall, a wall of a city that had not been seen or touched for four hundred years. It was the first major new Incan find since 1911.

There are explorers who spend lifetimes in the search for such a discovery and never realize their goal. We were lucky. The *In Seach Of . . .* crew had made a major find the first time out. We take no special credit. We were along for the ride. The laurels belong to Professor Edmundo Guillen, a Peruvian archeologist.

His quest was the famed Vilcabamba. According to legend, the last Incan ruler, Tupac Amaru, withdrew to Vilcabamba in the face of the Spanish onslaught. There the Inca nation made its final stand. From the day of the Conquistadores, it was believed that an enormous trove of gold and silver was carried to Vilcabamba by the Incas. The city, however, could not be found. It was lost. For almost four centuries adventurers and explorers, armed with the slimmest of accounts, launched expeditions into the foreboding jungles of the territory in east central Peru generically called Vilcabamba.

The belief that a lost city existed gave rise to the legends of El Dorado. For four hundred years the jungles of Peru were scoured for the actual fortress of Tupac Amaru. If found, it was believed that the city would yield untold treasure.

A startling announcement was made in 1911. Harvard's Hiram Bingham electrified the world of Incan archeology. He claimed that he had discovered Vilcabamba. What he found in fact was Machu Picchu, a wondrous fortress perched on a mountaintop. While Bingham asserted as late as 1951 that his discovery was Vilcabamba, other historians declared that the splendors of Machu Picchu did not fit historical accounts of Spanish expeditions to Vilcabamba in the mid-sixteenth century,

According to the ancient tale, Vilcabamba lay in rich pastureland in a valley four miles wide by two in length. Machu Picchu, placed on the pinpoint of a mountain, hardly matched the description.

The lure of Vilcabamba drew Dr. Edmundo Guillen to the quest. He is a professor of archeology at the University of San Marco and a specialist in sixteenth-century Peruvian history.

Polish archeologist Elzbieta Dzukowska, joined Professor Guillen in the hunt for the real Vilcabamba. The method he used was to construct, from letters and personal descriptions of the city, a portrait of the entire region surrounding Vilcabamba as it was seen in the mid 1570s. For ten years Guillen participated in aerial surveys of the Vilcabamba region, piecing together significant landmarks from the early accounts with parallel landmarks that exist today.

In April 1973 he had narrowed the field to a valley in the Vilcabamba region that was some ten miles long. It took until mid-summer of 1976 for Dr. Guillen to decide that he could, armed with maps created from four-hundred-year-old accounts, find a city that fell to the soldiers of Spain in 1572. *In Seach Of . . .* cameraman Tony Halik joined the expedition that would take twelve gruelling days of hacking paths through the jungle, and on the twelfth day, July 22, 1976, the machete cleaved through a vine and rang loudly against the wall of Vilcabamba. Dr. Guillen had made the most important archeological discovery in Peru in more than half a century, and we were there. There is no thrill to match the moment of discovery.

The actual work of excavating Vilcabamba from the overgrowth of four hundred years of jungle greenery will take months, even years. The city has an area of some five kilometers and nearby a cave that contains what may be the most fascinating of all Guillen's discoveries—the cave of the dead king.

The Inca buried their last leader somewhere near Vilcabamba. If the treasure exists, carried deep into the jungle to be hidden from the Spanish invaders, it would be in this cave at Vilcabamba. Dr. Guillen knows it will take months of labor to excavate the sealing stone, the great boulder that was lodged over the burial chamber to prevent the encroachment of grave robbers.

Looking at the pictures, I feel the prickle of excitement of discovery. I discovered the true essence of why we launch each of our searches for lost civilizations. In the moment of discovery I found myself linked directly to the past, fused, as it were, to humanity that was more than four hundred years old. I was a part of the past, as much as the past is a part of me, and so I was prepared to launch the quest around the world for other lost civilizations.

# 1

# Where Did Everyone Go?

All dead cities are inhabited by some kind of ghosts, I think.

Clairvoyants sometimes claim to see these ghosts. Investigators of psychic phenomena talk of long-lasting "emanations"—invisible imprints left behind by happenings in a specific place. This might be. A room often stays warm after embers are cold in the fireplace. Scents linger when their source is gone. Caverns reverberate. Can thought waves do something similar?

I'm not psychic. I don't see ghosts. But when I wander through lonely ruins in far places of the world, something nudges my brain. Images crowd in. I look at a crumbled stone stairway and I imagine the courtiers and priests who climbed it. I look at a weed-grown tile court worked with images of mythical beasts, and I think I feel what the artisans felt when they laid the tiles a few millennia ago.

Lord Byron, the nineteenth-century poet, may have

sensed a wraith at his elbow when he walked in the moonlight in a deserted city and wrote:

> So we'll go no more a-roving
> So late into the night,
> Though the heart be still as loving,
> And the moon be still as bright.

I think he knew, somehow, what it had been like on that long-dead avenue some summer evening when the late strollers were still out and music murmured faintly somewhere, but there was a premonition of an era ending:

> For the sword outwears its sheath,
> And the soul wears out the breast,
> And the heart must pause to breathe,
> And love itself have rest.
>
> Though the night was made for loving,
> And the day returns too soon,
> Yet we'll go no more a-roving
> By the light of the moon.

Perhaps it was Byron who started me on the search I'm going to tell you about in this book. Some of his poems set me tingling like a tuning fork.

The thought of civilizations wearing out was a theme that haunted Byron and came to haunt me. The grandeur and desolation of history, the hint of evil behind stone facades, the thunder of imperial names dying away into everlasting silence—Byron felt deeply about them. He had an eerie way of visualizing the end of empires, and some of his visions were partly confirmed afterward by archaeologists' discoveries.

For example, in 1815 he wrote "The Destruction of Sennacherib," a vivid description of a plague that suddenly attacked the Assyrian king Sennacherib's mighty army while it was besieging Jerusalem, as implied briefly in the Bible: "That night the angel of the Lord went out, and smote in the camp of the Assyrians . . . and in the morning, behold, they were all dead." (II Kings 19:35–36) Thirty years later, a young novice in archaeology, Henry Layard, dug into a mound on the Tigris River and found an obelisk covered with cuneiform script. At that time, no one in the world could read cuneiform. The deepest scholars knew no more about Assyria than the Old Testament told, which they assumed was mainly fiction. Only later, when the text was translated, did the obelisk tell its tale of bloody conquest in Palestine, ending when a half-mad Sennacherib abruptly broke off on the verge of taking the country's last stronghold, Jerusalem. What made him stop? The obelisk did not say. But finally, in 1938, another archaeologist, James Lesley Starkey, dug up a mass grave in the rock near Jerusalem with two thousand uninjured human skeletons, obviously dumped in with desperate haste. Since there was one such burial pit, others might be near. The evidence pointed to a raging epidemic in Sennacherib's army, as Byron had imagined.

Likewise, long before there was proof that the biblical city of Nineveh had actually existed, Byron conjured up a narrative of its last moments. He described a great tyrant, Sardanapalus, in a magnificent palace. In the climactic episode, the extravagant old dynast foresees the fulfillment of an ancient prophecy that his capital will collapse, so he gathers his harem, his slaves, his dogs, and his horses—and orders them murdered in his presence before igniting his own funeral pyre. The French painter Eugene Delacroix borrowed Byron's slaughter scene for one of his most sensational canvases, *The Death of Sardanapalus*.

Just who Sardanapalus may have been has never been established, although vague Greek gossip told of a king by that name, apparently confused with Ashurbanipal—whose palace with its great library of tablets came to light when Nineveh's ruins were finally found. We now know that Ashurbanipal, his wives, and his treasures were burned in the year 880 B.C.

Anyhow, I came to share the fascination that Byron, Delacroix, Shelley, and other romantics of that period felt for royal names from the invisible past—some names perhaps imaginary, some handed down through the Bible or persistent myths. The names evoked drumbeats, fanfare of trumpets, and clanging cymbals: Nebuchadnezzar. Belshazzar. Ozymandias. Herod. Hammurabi. Harun al-Rashid. Angkor Wat. Wassukkanni. Quetzalcoatl. Sargon. Priam. Minos. Zeus. Camelot.

Do those strange names hit you like sledgehammers? I felt an impact when I read them and whispered them to myself. I had to know about them. I had to go where emanations from them might still hang in the air like invisible storm clouds over sun-smitten ruins in the wilderness.

Fortunately, I happen to be in the business of producing documentary films for television. Therefore, I can choose my own topics. I can go with researchers and camera crews to any place on earth where a hunch tells me I'll find a good story.

Now I felt a compulsion to go in search of answers to some great mysteries of antiquity: What made a civilization vanish? What made thousands of city dwellers flee from (or perhaps die in) a splendid city that looked to be at the height of its grandeur? Where did they go?

And when they went, why did silence fall, seemingly, instead of a spreading ripple of folk tales from wherever they took refuge?

So long after the fact, answers to such questions might not be possible. But I would search.

And what about the broad question underlying these others: Was there a common pattern woven into massive disasters scattered across thousands of years?

The most sublime machinery on earth, civilization itself, seemed to have a way of popping into view rather suddenly here or there, only to be wrecked sooner or later. What could I learn from the wreckage?

In some lost empires, I gathered, there had been tyranny like Hitler's, so rigid and terrifying that nations finally rose against it rather than compromise, whereupon the tyrants hurled themselves on their enemies and were shattered. But this was not always the story. Some majestic, far-flung societies endured for thousands of years, only to be undermined at last by dark forces working from within, or obliterated from outside by catastrophe—sometimes a catastrophe that prophets foretold, if various documents are to be trusted. But were there deeper causes? Did the strangely diverse list of dead cities and states share some fatal flaw—perhaps a flaw to be found in our own civilization as well?

At any rate, tales of terrible, mysterious downfalls had to be dramatic. They should make television material. So I determined to investigate.

One of the first facts I found, in a general scanning of the field, was one I'd half known but never fully grasped. Maybe it will help you, as it did me, to see mankind's long confused story more clearly.

Do you realize that as recently as the time of Byron and his contemporaries—even as recently as our great-grandfathers' day, in most cases—human knowledge of ancient history was just a few scraps?

Our forefathers spoke with certitude of "the dawn of civilization" and "the dawn of history." They were sure just when both dawns had come. Very comfortable they must have been to stand, as they thought, at the high noon of human progress, and glance back to watch the epochs of the past click into sight like a reversed chronometer, until the dial went blank in the small hours. Seen that way, it was quite tidy and gave an admirable stability to existence in the best of all possible worlds.

The vastly learned archbishop James Ussher, by laborious calculations based on data in the Holy Scriptures, fixed the time when God said "Let there be light" as a certain Sunday morning in April of the year 4004 B.C. His timetable was considered authoritative enough to be set in the margins of reference editions of the authorized version of the Bible.

With this as a guideline, only two dawns were recognized as such: the daybreak of living creatures in the Holy Land, and the sunrise of civilization in classical Greece. Only a few antiquaries fussed about other dawns known to have shone in China and Egypt; these were clearly meant by the Great Clockmaker to be no more than glimmerings during some vague breakfast hour.

We needn't laugh. Earlier civilizations were also interested in the past, but took even more limited views of it. Egypt handed down its own history reverently from its beginnings at about 3000 B.C., yet never seemed to suspect that anything had happened earlier. Greece had a word for the discussion of antiquities, from which we derive our word *archaeology*. But as late as the fifth century B.C., Thucydides, most reliable of ancient historians, confidently remarked that no history worth recording had occurred before his own time.

Lately this neat little horizon has widened awesomely. We see a timetable that keeps regressing. By 1860 the dawn of Genesis, as dated by Ussher, was known to be much too late. Behind it was the dawn of Assyria, and behind that the dawn of Babylon, and behind that Sumer, a world of cities that rimmed the Persian Gulf from the Tigris to the Euphrates. Sumer was especially shocking to biblical scholars because it contained clay tablets telling a flood story much like that of Noah and the Ark, which, according to the Book of Genesis, was supposed to have occurred a thousand years earlier.

Thus, the "dawn of civilization" is slipping farther and farther back, already displacing all the darkness back to midnight. No sooner do we accustom ourselves to an earlier dawn than another brightens behind it, and we wonder how long this bewildering rearward progression really may be.

Consider what happened near Jericho, where an archaeological expedition began unearthing a walled city that medieval Turks had called Çatal Hüyük. As the diggers went down, they found city beneath city until there were twelve, each abandoned in turn and covered by a new city atop it. Any one of these might be thought worth a "dawn of civilization" label, for they showed signs of luxury and complex administration, with frescoes and tools and metalwork.

The oldest and lowest of these cities was dated at

about 8000 B.C. Yet, the expedition is sure that even older cities lie below, still hidden for lack of time and money to excavate them. Finding the record of civilized mankind is like peeling an onion, layer after layer.

We "moderns" aren't yet at ease with all these layers or false dawns or whatever we may call them. Sometimes we get an impression of strange and distant people whose ways were mostly different from our own. The only dawns we feel really pleased to contemplate are those with which we can connect ourselves, and from which the passage of sunny civilization to our own time has been understandable and almost unbroken.

Nevertheless, uneasy as we may be, it's exciting to see aspects of the distant past that have been lost for millennia. The revelation that so much of man's accomplishment and thought, his dreams along with his doings, is buried somewhere gives us a shock that has been felt over and over again during the last four or five generations.

I asked myself, How much more is still buried? Maybe we've found almost all that will ever be found. Maybe the rest has been worn down and wiped out altogether.

Well, let's see what geology and anthropology say, inexact as that may be.

In Dr. Jacob Bronowski's *The Ascent of Man,* which you may have seen on television, he takes us back fifty million years "in very round figures" to a fossil lemur; jumps twenty million years to a skull found in Egypt with "ape-like teeth," then skips on ten million more years to "anthropoid apes." And then the story really bothers me. He says:

> And there is now a blank in the fossil record of five to ten million years. Inevitably the blank hides the most intriguing part of the story, when . . . man is firmly separated from . . . the modern apes. But we have found no unequivocal record of that yet.

Notice the last sentence. It nonchalantly skims across a yawning credibility gap. It is like an alchemist telling us that a base metal has been transmuted to gold, although no trace of the actual process of transmutation has been found yet.

What do we have at this point? A half-dozen skulls spanning a period of fifty million years, on which science spins a story of man's ascent from apes? Dr. Bronowski goes on, "Two million years ago we were not yet men. One million years ago we were." I presume these too are very round figures.

What else happened on earth during those last few million years? Look first at the most recent geologic happenings.

The great ice layer, often thousands of feet thick, capable of grinding up mountains and compressing the rocks beneath with a force of seven tons per square foot, made its most recent retreat between eight and twelve thousand years ago. Before its advance were hundreds of thousands of years of mild climate. If there were civilizations during that long, long time, the last glaciers could have scoured away all traces of them.

Look back further. In the last 600,000 years, the Great Cold came four times and went away four times, in cyclic rotation. If there were men, as the anthropologists believe, what were they doing during those ice ages or in between them? We have almost no clues. For all we know, they may have gone from barbarism to a golden age and back a hundred times.

Look back further yet. Before the first of the four great glacial periods, there were no ice sheets for a hundred million years. Science says there were no men then—which means only that no traces of men have been found.

Whether there were men or not, that hundred-million-year chapter in Earth's history, basking in sunshine, must have been a peculiar one. Why did the chapter end? Why did glaciers arise on a hot planet?

Astronomers say the sun was essentially constant during that period, and so was Earth's orbit—no swerves or speed-ups that would produce hot epochs, no lags that would cause temperature drops. But astronomer Fred Hoyle theorizes that the unusual occurrence that ended the hundred-million-year summer was the breakup of comets, showering tiny fragments of debris into our atmosphere. These particles piercing the highest cloud layer would probably cause condensation there, followed by precipitation—a probability familiar to us ever since our first experiments with cloud seeding to make rain. Then, if all the vast topmost cloud layer turned to rain or snow, it might destroy the protective film of vapor that prevents heat from escaping, as if the planet had thrown off its warm blanket. This could get glaciers started. Thereafter, the slow hydrologic processes of melting and refreezing could make the ice mountains advance and retreat every few hundred thousand years.

Man was very slow in blooming, if Dr. Bronowski and his colleagues are right. For most of his first million years he progressed very little. He emerged from his Stone Age only about ten thousand years ago. I wonder . . .

What is ten thousand years on a planet at least five billion years old? Some forms of life arose here between two and three billion years ago, to judge from the scanty available evidence. Since then, just in the last million years, when we're sure man existed, deep rifts opened and closed, mountains rose and crumbled, coastlines pushed out and were eaten away, seas drained and refilled and overflowed. Did cities rise and tumble too, leaving nothing that survived those huge geologic changes? We'll never know, perhaps.

Even so, there's much we can find out.

As we look back to the earliest known civilizations, our distant view tends to foreshorten the course of events. To put them in perspective, imagine a tape on which everything that happened from the time of Columbus to ourselves has been recorded on the last three inches. To scan the tape back to the date of the first known cave paintings, we'd have to stretch it out fifty-five feet.

It's on that long strip of tape that we still may be

able to narrow the long blanks and fill in sketchy parts prior to the last few inches. Countless hunks of history may still lie buried under the debris of our time.

Or think another way. Suppose that the whole existence of man has been compressed into twelve hours, and we are living at noon of the long human day. Be conservative and assume that man has walked upright and thought creatively for only 240,000 years. Each hour of our clock would then represent 20,000 years. Each minute equals 333 years. For more than eleven and a half hours nothing was recorded. We know of no persons or events, but we infer that man was here, for we find stone tools, bits of pottery, and pictures of mammoths and bison.

Not until 11:40 did the first signs of Egyptian and Babylonian civilizations begin to appear. Classical Greece, which we customarily call ancient, arose about 11:53. At 11:59; Sir Francis Bacon wrote his monumental *Advancement of Learning*. A half minute ago, man invented steam engines and began the industrial revolution. A second ago, he flew to the moon.

But the hour between eleven and twelve o'clock doesn't look as empty to us as it did to our forefathers. In the world of archaeology, the last few decades have been an age of exploration as rich in adventure and discovery as was the age of Columbus and Magellan.

Reports have come in from windy uplands of Anatolia, where a strange people, the Hittites, once ruled with formidable authority; from flowery jungles of Cambodia, where some unsung genius raised temples of dazzling and exotic beauty for the Khmers; from Central American rain forests, where the remains of white temple cities could be the work of Israel's lost tribes; from the shores of the Aegean, where the fabulous myths of our own classical past suddenly proved true.

The pick-and-shovel brigades have invaded Gibeon, where once the sun stood still for Joshua; they are groping for the ruins of Gordium, capital of Phrygia, where King Midas saw concubines turn to gold at his touch. The great Tower of Babel, the labyrinth of the Minotaur, the magnificent hanging gardens of

Babylon, and other wonders from an unlikely past are taking the shape of historical reality.

The city of Ephesus, sacred to the goddess Artemis, and Aphrodisias, sacred to Aphrodite, are yielding their ancient secrets. Remnants of Hatra, razed long ago by the Persians, are being pieced together. Samarra, that lovely capital of caliphs who ruled the Near East during Europe's Dark Ages, is emerging from the dust. With the Bible's help, searchers have found more than a thousand ancient sites in Transjordan and have set a firmer date for the Exodus; they have located the long-lost mines of King Solomon and spotted the site of his port on the Red Sea.

Everywhere archaeologists, armed with modern science, are lengthening and widening history's view. Aerial cameras find the faint outlines of long-gone walls and canals. Magnetometers ferret out forgotten fortifications. Carbon-14 dating is causing consternation in museums by establishing accurate ages of artifacts back beyond any written record. Ultraviolet light irradiates reused writing materials called palimpsests, and shows words that were erased thousands of years ago.

Well, I'm no archaeologist except in a very amateur, unscientific way. But maybe there's a side of archaeology that is more a matter of discerning and imagining than of digging and measuring. Maybe there's an art of seeing a whole camp site in a broken shard of pottery on the dull gray desert. Maybe there's an ability to hold a relic in the hand and hear in the mind's ear an echo of a forgotten language almost understood.

I wanted to see if I had such a sixth sense—to visit the places where civilizations had gone down in darkness, and ascertain whether I could feel or see anything there. I would put my trusty researchers to work, deploy my camera crews, and come back with a television series.

Where was the logical place to go first? Where was the first known civilization?

# 2

# The Drowned Kingdoms

My researchers felt that Atlantis would be the place to start, but I disagreed. So many books had been written about it, but there was not a scrap of solid proof in any of them. But my researchers strongly supported the theory that Atlantis may have been the first great empire, the fountainhead for other civilizations. I had to admit that the theory might account for some curious facts, like the blue-eyed, blond tribesmen in the North African mountains; like the Basque language, which is so different from all others; like rabbits in the Azores, where the theory of evolution says they can't be; like beetles common only to Africa, America, and the Mediterranean region.

Examined more closely, the theory implies that sometime there must have been big islands where none are now. Geologists and oceanographers agree. There are underwater mountains and mesas in every ocean. Call them lost continents—Mu, or Lemuria, or Atlantis, whatever you like. The only trouble is, I argued, they've been submerged for at least twenty thousand years, maybe much longer. Even ten thousand years ago there were absolutely no cities, just Stone Age nomad hunters, according to the archaeological evidence. So if Atlantis had those blonds and beetles and rabbits, so what? My opinion was that it didn't have a civilization. To me, starting there would be like starting in Never-Never Land or El Dorado or the wonderful Kingdom of Oz. We'd be starting with pure fiction.

Of course I'd read Plato—the one and only written source for the Atlantis story. He told of a mighty seafaring people who lived beyond the Strait of Gibraltar on a mountainous continent bigger than North Africa and Asia combined—800,000 square miles, by his figures.

He said that the capital city was far grander and richer than Athens, with aqueducts and baths, bridges and docks and naval stores, and temples in which sacred bulls ran loose. They were "the fairest and noblest race of men who ever lived . . . but when the divine part began to fade away, they then behaved unseemly and grew visibly debased, full of avarice and unrighteous power." Therefore, Zeus decided to punish them, and "in a single day and night the island of Atlantis disappeared under the sea."

How did Plato know all this?

By hearsay. According to him, the story came from the great Athenian law-giver, Solon, who had served as high magistrate for twenty-two years, then retired in 572 B.C. and spent ten years in Egypt—long before Plato was born.

Solon too got the tale by hearsay (through interpreters) from Egyptian priests who claimed they had been handing it down verbally for a dim nine thousand years. He supposedly made notes and began to write it as an epic poem, which he never finished. No such writings were found by his family.

In fact, nothing else in ancient literature says in plain language that an island civilization sank beneath the sea. Solon returned to Athens as an old man and told the Atlantis tale to his brother—from whom it was passed along through 150 years to the brother's great-grandson, Critias, whom Plato quotes as telling the story in old age. Many other Greek writers quoted Solon, but not about Atlantis, as far as we can tell from the surviving scrolls.

Not reassuring, was it? You know how stories get garbled and magnified by word-of-mouth. On the other hand, Plato himself probably visited Egypt and could have picked up the Atlantis legend there. Why didn't he tell it on his own authority? Because first-person stories just weren't his style. He never mentioned himself in any of his writings. He put them all into the form of conversations between students and Socrates or other mentors.

He may have chosen a long-dead source in order to protect himself from accusations that he made up the Atlantis story. Fiction is more interesting when it purports to be a true story based on conveniently missing "notes" or "an old manuscript." This device is dear to the hearts of fantasy writers from Horace Walpole down to Jules Verne and Edgar Allan Poe.

We know for sure that Plato had a fertile imagination. His writings included descriptions of islands floating in the sky, of Tartarus below Hades inside the earth, of primeval men with four arms and four legs. This was why I'd always suspected that Plato personally invented Atlantis and its destruction by earthquake and flood. His skeptical pupil Aristotle was quoted as saying "he who invented Atlantis also destroyed it."

By the time Plato put forth the Atlantis yarn he was in his seventies and had gone through a lot—including enslavement and liberation, a reign of terror in Athens, competitive wrestling, a battle with the Delians, which brought him a decoration for bravery, an abortive attempt to apply his theories of government at the court of the tyrant Dionysus, and forty years of schoolteaching. Significantly, Plato's prescription for an ideal government, expounded in the *Republic* long before he wrote about Atlantis, is almost identical, word for word, to the political system described as an actuality in his Atlantis dialogue.

His physical description of Atlantis conflicted

with facts discovered later. According to his dimensions, the continent would have been too big to fit into either the Mediterranean or the Aegean, which were the seas around which civilization had centered in classical times. In the Atlantic Ocean—named after his legendary land—undersea explorers had no more luck than did Magellan or Columbus in finding vestiges of the continent Plato described.

The likeliest location seemed Galicia Bank, a flat-topped bulge twenty miles long, lying a half mile deep off the northwest corner of Spain. In 1958, the British research vessel *Discovery II* dredged the bank and took hundreds of underwater photos, finding nothing. No bits of pottery or tools, no signs of a drowned civilization. More recently, Dr. Maurice Ewing of Columbia University announced that after thirteen years of probing the mid-Atlantic ridge he hadn't located any clues to sunken cities—even though he'd taken soundings, combed with dredges, and plunged cameras and searchlights as deep as three miles.

The "day and a night" during which Atlantis supposedly sank would have been somewhere around 9600 B.C., as Plato told it. But if the highly civilized survivors fled to other lands—there must have been some at sea in ships when the land sank—why didn't scholars find clues to their existence? Egypt itself, where the priests supposedly had been handing down the facts ever since the cataclysm, wasn't even crudely civilized until about 4000 B.C., as far as scientists knew. Archaeologists all over the world were sure that mankind everywhere was just beginning to emerge from caves during the Stone Age nine or ten thousand years B.C., and that the transition from wandering hunters to settled farmers took many centuries. So Plato's date seemed wildly wrong.

Whatever the date, could a whole continent sink far from sight in a day and a night? Geologists say that during the height of the last Ice Age, some twenty thousand years ago, so much water was locked up in glaciers and polar ice that the ocean levels might have been five hundred feet lower than they are now. So when the ice mountains melted and the oceans rose, any number of kingdoms could have been flooded. But the sea level inched up over a long period, apparently.

I pointed all this out to my associates, but they kept defending the Atlantis idea, pointing out that Plato had heard and written other fantastic tales that had turned out to be true—like the one about the faraway continent where he said daylight lasted for a whole month during the summer (this was long before the Arctic and Antarctic were discovered).

One of my researchers suggested that perhaps the empire of Atlantis arose about 11,000 B.C., peaked in 10,000, and fell in 9500. If the survivors reverted to barbarism after a few centuries, this would fit in with the Stone Age chronology.

The others agreed. Another of my associates pointed out that the ancient Greeks surmised that humanity went through cycles of culture and savagery, like the Dark Ages after Rome fell. Aristotle and Democritus and many other Greek writers wondered if everything had been invented and lost innumerable times. Aristotle wrote in his *Metaphysics:* "Probably each art and each science has often been developed as far as possible and has again perished."

The theory fascinated me, but I couldn't see how we could illustrate it on television. If Atlantis was destroyed ten thousand years ago, and there's nothing on Earth indicating a civilization that old, where would we send our camera crews?

My associates had a solution. We could send them to quite a few places, if we went on the premise that Atlantis fell later instead of earlier. We could suppose that Plato—or Solon—saw Egyptian writings about Atlantis, and that he misread the Egyptian symbol for "hundred" as "thousand," thereby multiplying all figures tenfold. If we eliminated that extra zero, Atlantis would become eighty thousand square miles in area, which would fit several areas not very deep under water. The date of the cataclysm would become nine *centuries* before Solon instead of nine thousand years. This would put it in the fifteenth century B.C., when Egypt did exist.

Maybe that was the answer. I asked them to check further and develop a list of likely locations.

It turned out that there were three sites of undersea exploration where sunken cities seem to be. One was in the Bahamas, one in the Aegean between present-day Turkey and Greece, and one in shallow waters off Spain, west of the Straits of Gibraltar.

We had photographed underwater ruins in the Bahamas a few years earlier, for a TV documentary called *In Search of Ancient Mysteries* (see my book of the same title). But I decided to take another look. Divers were still making discoveries there—and an occult prediction about the area seemed to be coming true.

In 1940, Edgar Cayce, the "sleeping prophet," had predicted in a trance that part of Atlantis would rise from the sea thereabouts. He had even set an approximate date—1968 or 1969. In those years, aircraft pilots did begin to report glimpses of what looked like rectangular enclosures, or the foundations of big buildings, under the water. Maybe the sea bottom was rising.

I knew that there were massive walls off the shore of Bimini—I'd seen them. But this time, maybe I could see more.

The seven-hundred-odd Bahama Islands are scattered across ninety thousand square miles of sunlit solitude in the North Atlantic basin, starting near the coast of Florida and running southeast almost to Haiti. The whole Bahama Banks area is fairly shallow, and might have been above water five or ten thousand years ago.

I put on a diver's mask and slipped under the glistening surface layers of light, sank down to the bottom, and wandered among the huge white blocks that the pilots had seen and the divers had studied. They were as square-cut and as smoothly fitted as parts of a modern edifice. They extended far beyond my sight, fading into the opalescent haze. Were they paved causeways, or plazas, or the tops of buried walls? I couldn't see enough to guess. Even the divers weren't sure, because drifting sand kept burying some parts and exposing others.

A deserted city might lie there, extending for miles among the coral and swaying seaweed. If so, the city was not recorded in any history that has thus far come to light. I knew that divers had brought up pottery and figurines that no museum was willing to classify as typical of a known culture. I knew that Pino Tarolla, one of the world's leading undersea researchers, had found a marble column that could be part of a temple or villa. He believed it was twelve thousand years old. Maybe scientific tests would fix a date for it.

Suppose there had been a civilization on the Bahama Banks. What became of it? Rather than simply moving to the higher ground that still shoulders up from the sea as islands, all the people must have been drowned, or must have fled far away. When Columbus reached those islands he found no stonework, no civilization—only primitive Indians in huts. Plato said that the Atlanteans were warned of impending disaster, and he implied that some escaped.

An Atlantis theory could explain those well-engineered stone structures in thirty-five feet of water. It might also explain what had been found under a sunken ship.

The ship had gone down in 1830. But it had crushed something beneath it that was more interesting: the remains of a smaller, much older ship. Studying the fragments, experts decided that this ancient ship was a typical vessel of the Phoenicians, those sea wanderers who built a vast network of small seaport towns.

The Phoenicians seemed rather uncanny and mysterious to the Mediterranean peoples, who could not understand how this tiny race could be so widespread. The Phoenician empire depended not on vast territories but on a fleet, a system of forts, and the good will of its customers. The Phoenicians had no army and no strong war galleys, but they had footholds on the Spanish and North African coasts, on the

Bosporus, and in Italy and Sicily. Their agents were seen with the priests and pharaohs of Egypt, with the kings of Persia and Babylon and Assyria. They were in every port, but said little. They arrived, transacted business with memorable honesty, and disappeared again. They offered wares purveyed by no other nation, and sometimes hinted that they had traveled to lands unknown in the Mediterranean.

What had a Phoenician ship been doing so near the then undiscovered American continents?

At some time in the dim past, we know from historic clues, a few bold sea adventurers did move west into the broad Atlantic in search of a fabled continent. These men, mostly Phoenicians, left no record of finding Atlantis. But they found the Madeiras and the Canary Islands. And wherever they wandered, gossip sprang up of other island kingdoms west over the ocean—the Hesperides, where grew the golden apples, the Fortunate Islands, the Isles of the Blest, and somewhere out there the Elysian Fields, which became the abode of the blessed in Greek mythology. Perhaps legends like these led the Vikings to America about 1000 A.D.

But I was peering much further back. If venturesome early Phoenicians were in the Bahamas three thousand years ago, were they visiting the western edge of a continent of Atlantis? Plato's description, taken literally, would mean that part of the Atlantic was once occupied by a land mass linking the Mediterranean area to the Caribbean area. If the Bahamas were the western or Caribbean tip of this trans-Atlantic land bridge, where was the Mediterranean tip?

Somewhere off Spain? The broken remains of a city had recently been reported on the sea bottom near Cadiz—an old, old city that was originally the Phoenician port of Gades.

I took a little time to read up on the theory of continental drift, since this might fit our Atlantean jigsaw puzzle. As recently as twelve years ago, the idea that continents moved and that oceans were widening was so radical that geologists scorned it as "geopoetry."

Theoretical calculations showed it to be highly improbable. What mighty mechanism could move continents?

Today, the great majority of earth scientists are convinced that the whole skin of the earth is in slow but fairly constant motion; that continents are made of lighter materials than are the ocean floors, and are drifting like rafts on a bog. It now appears that they have moved at a rate of an inch or two per year throughout nearly all the earth's history.

This revolution in thinking really began a century ago when a few imaginative people noticed the remarkably similar coastlines on opposite sides of the Atlantic. They speculated that early in its history the earth's crust had broken and the continents had moved apart.

Alfred Wegener, a brilliant young German, happened to read a description of close resemblances between some animals of Africa and South America. From this and other data, he theorized that the present continents are drifted fragments of one colossal land that broke up during the era when the first dinosaurs began to roam the jungles. He suggested that great mountain chains were pushed up by compression between colliding continents. His colleagues only chuckled.

However, after World War II, new scientific instruments brought a flood of information about the structure of our planet. They discovered a forty-thousand-mile submarine mountain range. By sonar they plumbed a great abyss in the western Pacific, the six-mile-deep Mariana Trench, in which the highest mountains could be sunk without a trace. Other huge trenches were found at many places in the Pacific—but not in the Atlantic.

Studying the magnetic fields frozen in lava, geophysicists found that lavas about 200 million years old pointed to a north pole at a location dramatically different from the present pole. Lavas of other ages showed other pole positions. "Polar wandering curves" for each continent were charted. The European and American polar wandering curves fit together. The logical explanation was that Europe and America had been together about 200 million years ago. If they had been inching apart ever since at a rate of a yard or two per century, this would account for the present distance between them. Later evidence indicated that Africa and South America were together about 150 million years ago.

Earth's crust, floating on the yielding molten rock deep below, isn't the rigid layer that it seems. The crust has slipped or slid around the interior like the shell of an egg. It cracks and buckles, very slowly, with pieces of crust sliding over or under one another. Glaciers depress parts of the surface, which slowly rise again after the ice melts.

Cores from the sea floor confirmed this view. Lately scientists had been eyeing Antarctica, wondering if it crept south after a massive upheaval in comparatively recent times. Conceivably, part of what is now the South Pole region could have been underpinning for an Atlantis that stretched from somewhere in the Bahamas to somewhere near Spain.

So I had to investigate Spain.

That country's geographical position is peculiar. Thrusting massively out of Europe's southwestern corner, separated from Africa by only eight miles of easily crossed sea, it closes off the Mediterranean from the Atlantic Ocean. It faces Asia across the inland sea, whose shores saw the dawn of our civilization. Into it from all directions came prehistoric tribes, Celts, Phoenicians, and their many successors.

In the north of Spain, certain shadowy wanderers settled in the Pyrenees to become the ancestors of the Basques, a race with a language whose roots still mystify philologists. (Oddly, Basques are good seamen despite their mountain homes. Many go down to the coast and ship out on fishing trawlers. Every year there are Basque skippers in the Atlantic sailing races.)

In Andalusia, in the south, other people arrived from somewhere—probably Morocco—bringing skilled craftsmanship with them. Those people learned how to work bronze about 2000 B.C. and sold their work throughout the Mediterranean. This put Andalusia into the realm of legend as a land of fabulous wealth.

This lore fascinated me because Cadiz is in Andalusia, on the coast near the mouth of the Guadalquivir River. In that same river valley, probably, was the lost metropolis of Tartessus—which also may have been the biblical Tarshish, Jonah's destination. Ezekiel mentioned mysterious "ships of Tarshish" which sailed from the Gulf of Aqaba to the equally mysterious Ophir, and brought back "gold, and silver, ivory, and apes and peacocks" for King Solomon. (I Kings 10:22)

Were Tartessus and Tarshish the same or different places? Where were they? We know for sure only that they were in southern Spain. Herodotus told of a king who ruled over Tartessus, and therefore many have thought it was a country rather than merely a city. The country was rich—Strabo wrote of a river "with springs rich in silver" and other writers mentioned its "silver mountains." Those mountains are now known to be Spain's Sierra Morena.

About 500 B.C., Tartessus disappeared from sight so mysteriously that Plato was inspired—some say—to base his Atlantis myth on it. I wondered if the place had been a Phoenician capital. Wherever they settled, Phoenicians lived near the sea rather than inland. It seemed almost as if they mistrusted the firmness of the land. Their empire was elusive, founded less on settlements than on trading routes, and its chief manifestation was its fleet of fragile ships. Phoenician towns were walled settlements with watchtowers, barracks, and storehouses. Outsiders saw no visible pillars, marble faces, or brightly painted statues of gods, such as the Mediterranean peoples cherished.

The Phoenicians dropped from history when Alexander's armies overran the coasts. Away from water, these nomad people were like magicians deprived of their magic wands. Alexander hewed wooden crosses for two thousand of the men, and sold the women and children into slavery. It was an act calculated to show the world that the Phoenician sea lords had been conquered by him, the lord of the earth. He wiped them from history. The surviving Phoenicians melted away, like other peoples, mainly the Persians and the Carthaginians. Their only traces left to us were a few statues and a strange many-colored bust in sandstone, *The Lady of Elche,* carved in a strong and flowing Celtic style.

A town called Gades (which became the big city of Cadiz in the Spanish empire) was founded sometime before 800 B.C.—perhaps by Phoenicians, perhaps by Carthaginians. It may well have been a sort of suburb or satellite of Tartessus or Tarshish. German archaeologist Adolf Schulten wrote a book arguing that Tartessus was the key city of Atlantis. Near the mouth of the Guadalquivir he dug up blocks of masonry that, he thought, showed that two older cities had been there—one dating from about 3000 B.C., the other from about 1500 B.C.

The Bible said that Tarshish had a great fleet. Plato said that Atlantis had a great fleet. Some occultists like Cayce, who supposedly got information about Atlantis in trances, said that its civilization dabbled in black magic near the end—and a ring inscribed with what looked like a magical spell was found deep in the mud of the Guadalquivir estuary. The characters, never deciphered, consist of a single four-letter word repeated three times, in the manner of many mystical charms and runes.

Schulten couldn't dig far, because water kept seeping in. The rest of Tartessus-Tarshish (or Atlantis?) might lie deep in the ooze offshore of Cadiz and the river mouth.

The legend of the golden land of Tarshish lived on in a sort of afterglow for many centuries after the Romans left. An Arab commander described it to his troops on the eve of their first invasion of Spain in 712 A.D.:

> Maidens as handsome as houris, their necks glittering with innumerable pearls and jewels, their bodies clothed with tunics of costly silks and sprinkled with gold, are awaiting your arrival, reclining on soft couches in the sumptuous palaces of crowned lords and princes.

Yet I saw no traces of sumptuous palaces in Andalusia. When I first went there I found bare brown and violet mountains, with tiny whitewashed towns at their feet. The land contained no pre-Roman ruins. I drove along 140 miles of Mediterranean shore whose dun sand seemingly had never been used for anything more than beached fishing boats and drying nets. Later, a land boom transformed that ribbon of shore into the fashionable Costa del Sol.

Cadiz—as the Spaniards renamed Gades—contained little that hinted at its centuries as a Phoenician and Carthaginian colony. Its antique splendors must have been hidden by the rising sea. Dr. Maxine Asher thought so. In 1973 she organized an expedition to dive two and a half miles offshore.

Some of the diving was to be done by twenty-five students from Pepperdine University, which granted them summerschool credits. Dr. Asher is an energetic advocate of the theory that Atlantis is a discoverable reality.

"The trip with the students was the tenth I'd taken to Cadiz," Dr. Asher told me. "We were housed in government buildings. We had all the official permits and were given a welcoming party by government officials."

"So you'd already found something significant on earlier trips?"

"We'd been working with the only archaeological scuba diver of note in Spain, Francisco Salazar Casero—known as Paco. He identified four diving locations for us, about twenty miles north of Gibraltar. He'd found the remains of an ancient city at one of these sites. I have Paco's maps and sketches of huge walkways, walls, the whole thing."

"And this time what did you find?"

"Not much—because we began getting official and unofficial notices that we couldn't dive, couldn't go on the beach, couldn't go in the water. Generals and admirals at Gibraltar were countermanding the orders of the government in Madrid. We were stopped in an illegal way."

"But you didn't give up?"

"We decided to go ahead with our dive anyway, in secret. It was a decision by Dr. Egerton Sykes of England's Royal Anthropology Society, Dr. Rhoda Freeman of the Los Angeles school system, and myself. We selected our six best divers plus a United Press reporter, Stewart Slavin. One diver was an anthropologist. Another was chief photographer for the Irish Museum. The night before, Paco briefed them."

"They snuck out in the night?"

"In the middle of the night, they sneaked out and dived down ninety-five feet and took three rolls of film. The water was very murky, very sandy—you're now talking about the Atlantic, not the Caribbean. . . . They came back to the hotel and reported what they had found, this whole ancient site the same way Paco described it. We developed the film with five witnesses. To our bad luck, only one photo came out. It wasn't conclusive."

"So you tried again?"

"The divers went back on three successive days—but it stormed like a gale, for the first summer in twenty years, and they couldn't go into the water. By the fourth day, the police were all over the beaches."

"Did you ever learn why you were being chased out?"

"Yes, we heard later that there are United States nuclear submarines, missile bases, right there."

"How did it end?" I asked.

"We held a press conference, with dignitaries from the Spanish government, in a government building. All we said was, 'We believe we've found vestiges of Atlantis, subject to validation, which we firmly believe we can get.' The Cadiz newspaper used the one photo. The European newspapers gave us fantastic coverage. American papers smeared it, changed the whole story."

"You left Spain soon afterward?"

"Frightening things were going on in the hotel, to scare us out. Dr. Freeman and I decided we couldn't go on. I left for Ireland, and most of the students came too."

At first, I wondered why she had gone to Ireland.

But I could see a connection. Some Celtic tribes

had migrated to Ireland from Spain. And Celtic lore is full of tales of islands in the west, cities under the water. There are detailed legends about the Land of Youth, the Land of Fair Women, the islands of Weepers and of Hell, the Green-Island-under-the-Waves. Irishmen sometimes say they hear church bells ringing from the submerged cities.

Dr. Asher and her group found nothing more than did the ancient Irish monks, who sent six expeditions sailing west in skin-covered boats called curraghs to look for the legendary St. Brendan's Isle. State documents recorded those expeditions and specified how the land was to be distributed when found. The Irish believed that a medieval monk named Brendan went voyaging in search of the Earthly Paradise, which he'd heard was situated on a mid-Atlantic island. He found it, the legend said, after searching for seven years, during which he met demons, dragons, sea serpents, and other creatures resembling those described in Homer's *Odyssey*. St. Brendan's legend was so entrancing that it was translated into French, English, Welsh, and Spanish.

But I couldn't very well send camera crews groping for Atlantis through the Celtic twilight. Since the Spanish government's treatment of Dr. Asher indicated that we too would be stymied there, I headed instead for the Aegean Sea.

# 3

# The Wave that Wrecked a Civilization

The windy Aegean Sea is like a great lake, almost surrounded by land. Greece's jagged shores, on the mainland of Europe, lie to its west and north. To the east is the Asian part of Turkey. Along the south, like a breakwater, the long, narrow, mountainous island of Crete sets the Aegean apart from the rest of the Mediterranean Sea. South of Crete is nothing but ocean until you reach the coast of Africa—not a long voyage by modern standards, but in days when ships rarely sailed out of sight of a coast, it was enough to make the Aegean fairly remote from Egypt, the nearest civilized power from 3000 to 1000 B.C.

Myth said that a king named Aegeus once ruled over preclassical Athens. His son Theseus went to Crete and slew the Minotaur. On his return voyage, Theseus forgot to hoist white sails as the prearranged signal of success. The agonized King Aegeus saw the ship's black sails—the signal that Theseus was dead—whereupon he threw himself into the sea and drowned. It has been called the Aegean ever since. No one knows what it was called in the dim centuries before Greeks and Phoenicians, the centuries into which I now was questing.

I was bound for an island in the Aegean some seventy-eight miles northeast of Crete. It was one of two hundred twenty isles strewn in a great loose circle, and therefore called the Cyclades. They are mountain peaks of a land mass, now mostly drowned in the sea, that once linked the mainland with Asia Minor.

For centuries, beginning with the dawn of the Bronze Age about 3000 B.C., dwellers in the Cyclades had dominated the Mediterranean and outstripped Crete itself in commerce. The islanders were mining obsidian and trading in wheat, pottery, copper, and gems long before their neighbors in Crete or on the mainland. "Their weapons were of bronze, their houses of bronze, and they worked with bronze," the Greek poet Hesiod wrote of the men who lived thereabouts long before his own age. They slowly built up an elegant culture that would vanish suddenly, haunting the classical world, not to be found again until our own time.

My goal was the island that had been the crowning gem of this culture. The island was known by various names. Most people now call it Santorini, after its patron saint, Santa Irene. Legends gave it other names: Stronghyli, or Round Island, and Kalliste, or Most Fair. It has now been officially designated Thera, a name given to it by the classical Greeks.

Long ago Thera was a round, flowery island surrounding a conical mountain that rose a mile high from the sea. Today, most of this mountain is gone. As I stood at the rail of a motor launch I saw from afar what was left of Thera: a crescent-shaped mass with jagged ridges lancing into the sky. As we drew closer they loomed black and stark as battlements. The old island seemed a citadel under attack by the sea, with sloping rock sides that here threw back the surf and there had been breached.

Nearer yet, I saw cliff faces streaked with strata of black, white, pink, and rust red—marks of a turbulent past. From these strata, geologists deduced a brief terrible episode that had snuffed out civilization all around the Aegean. Now I was to see what archaeologists made of that same episode.

We landed at Thera from the west, within the incurve of its broken crescent. The curve was big—eighteen miles around the rim, and half enclosing some thirty square miles, according to the chart. It could have been a good harbor—except that it was far too deep. No ship's anchor could reach the bottom, thirteen hundred feet down. We had to tie up at a quay clinging tenaciously to the steep shore.

From there a cobbled path zigzagged upward like a staircase. A patient donkey carried me among whitewashed houses and steepled churches, up and up on a precarious climb that any sensible wild goat would have shunned. Santorini's donkeys were said to be inhabited by souls in purgatory, paying for their sins by toiling up that path.

I listened to the wind crying softly in the cliffs, watched the clouds—black as vultures—and pondered what this strange sharp-edged land had been fifteen centuries before Christ. On these steep slopes, along terraces like balconies, vineyards would have been lush with figs and olives and wine grapes. People would have been bathing in warm springs that bubbled from the sacred mountain in the center of the island, or steaming themselves in yellow-white vapor from its fissures.

My stony trail ended at a low wall beyond which was sheer space. The sea was so far below that its waves looked like wrinkles in gray silk. Gulls and terns hung before me, riding the wind that surged up the cliffs. Away to the north across wastes of water, the purple ghosts of mountains haunted the horizon. It was a fine view, and I wondered if it was the last view seen by some of Thera's ancient dwellers.

The wealthiest people and the government nabobs would have lived up here—or higher, perhaps, near a vanished summit. They could have looked down into the harbor that ringed the island. Many vessels would be lying at anchor, for in their time it was a good anchorage. The ships were one-masted, with square sails and seats for twenty paddlers on each side. In an epoch when competing powers in Egypt and Mesopotamia could design only banana-shaped vessels suitable for their rivers, ship builders in the Cyclades were using the keel, probably an Aegean invention. They sailed the Mediterranean from end to end, and even unloaded cargo at wharves on the Nile.

I imagined a day when the beautiful island-that-was lay basking in the sun. The tanned people in the crowded streets and cool villas were uneasy, for the shelflike streets intermittently shook beneath their feet. In the steambaths, the vapor was thickening into dense hot fog. Now and then deep rumbling came from below—perhaps, people said, roars of the sacred bulls that the gods reputedly penned in the underworld.

Thera's people probably didn't realize that they lived on the slopes of a mighty, slumbering volcano—as large or larger than Vesuvius or Etna. It was also an active earthquake zone. On that fateful day, the earth's jolts evidently opened subterranean cracks, through which cold sea water seeped into the lava furnace under the volcano. For a period of hours or days, steam and gas pressure rose steadily toward the bursting point.

Lava welled up and broke through. People on the slopes saw a river of red-hot rock creeping toward them. But there was a lull, giving everyone time to snatch up belongings and hasten downhill. Inside the mountain, the fiery fountain subsided awhile, seeping into a vast gas-filled chamber whose rock roof was riven with cracks.

At last, with a great deafening roar, the mountaintop blew apart. An enormous pillar of dust and vapor climbed into the sky. Soon the sky grew dark as night. A hot snowfall of powdery pumice and stones began. On the beach, everyone swam for the ships or scrambled into boats. But they were doomed.

If Thera was the fabled Atlantis, as some modern archaeologists believe, Plato's description of what happened could be literally true: "In a single day and night of misfortune . . . the island of Atlantis disappeared in the sea." Geological evidence proves that Thera underwent a volcanic eruption of maximum violence. When the volcano had spat out all its fiery core, the hollowed-out cone collapsed in on itself, falling into its lake of lava far below sea level. This suddenly opened a pit about forty-seven miles across and a quarter mile deep —sucking in approximately fifteen cubic miles of sea water.

After the downrush came the backwash, a spreading circle of water more than a hundred feet high, probably followed by others nearly as gigantic. The wave must have overturned all ships, drowned everyone on the Cyclades Islands except people in the mountains, and destroyed Crete's coastal cities. It raced across the Aegean and the eastern Mediterranean at more than a hundred miles an hour. Less than three hours later it engulfed the Egyptian delta, 450 miles away, where the children of Israel labored as slaves at the time. Afterward, it had enough force left to wipe out Syria's ancient port of Ugarit, tearing huge stone blocks from their foundations and scattering them like dice.

Just such a tidal wave might have caused Noah to take to his Ark. The suction in the sea and the subsequent outward wave (about twenty minutes later) might have given the Israelites their land path through the Red Sea, and might have crushed the pursuing Egyptians under the huge returning tidal wave. The iron-oxide fallout from Thera's explosion might have made the Nile run red. Certainly it blanketed the Jaffa shoreline, 562 miles away, with rosy pumice.

Egypt's Ten Plagues, as recorded in the Bible, might be explained by phenomena that accompany great volcanic eruptions. Whirlwinds, swamps, and red rain often are created by meteorological disturbances associated with eruptions, and there are aerial shock waves as destructive as those from a great bomb blast.

The Bible said that in Egypt the waters reddened, killing fish and driving frogs ashore. Darkness covered the land for three days. The wind roared. A fiery hail fell. Strong vapors destroyed what crops remained.

Egyptian documents confirmed the disaster. "The sun is veiled and shines not," said one papyrus. "O that the earth would cease from noise," lamented another.

Whether Egypt's plagues raged during the time of

Moses can't yet be confirmed or denied, because no contemporary evidence has been found. The Exodus took place during Solomon's reign, the Bible said, which was from 970 to 930 B.C. But the story of Moses was told to biblical scribes many centuries afterward, and could be incorrectly placed in time. It might have coincided with Thera's explosion, which scientists date at approximately 1520 B.C.

As for Thera, some of it sank into the newly opened undersea crater, and some was buried under thick layers of volcanic ash and powdered pumice (the frothy stuff formed when lava is suffused with gas bubbles). It was a dead island for centuries. Then Greek villagers came and settled. The first suspicion that a city lay under them arose during construction of the Suez Canal in the nineteenth century. Ash from there was known to make high-quality waterproof cement, so it was mined for the Suez project. French miners found that the layer of volcanic ash was a hundred feet thick in places. This implied the biggest volcanic eruption on record.

The French crews got curious and kept digging. Under tons of ash and pumice they found signs of a then-unknown civilization. Archaeologists visited, and burrowed into underground structures that were found to contain frescoes and pottery and artwork unlike anything from classical Greece. At that stage of archaeology, their age was unguessable.

A young Greek student of archaeology, Spyridon Marinatos, grew obsessed with curiosity about what had really happened on this bleak and sinister island. In 1932 he got a university grant of $135—a princely sum then—to excavate. He unearthed a small part of the old city, including a villa with glowing floral motifs. He found bronzes of a high quality, beautiful ceramics—including one of a bull, the Minoans' sacred beast—and ornate decorations in earth colors and crushed lapis lazuli.

Marinatos theorized that a huge eruption had destroyed much of the island and all its civilization. He was ignored by most of his colleagues. But in 1937 he became a visiting professor at the State University of

Utrecht, where he could delve into voluminous records of the 1883 Krakatau eruption in the Netherlands East Indies. That volcanic island burst with a roar heard 2,968 miles away. Volcanic dust hid the daylight for 275 miles around. The empty shell of the volcano slumped into a 600-foot-deep crater in the sea, making waves 120 feet high. The waves swept away entire towns and villages on the neighboring coasts of Java and Sumatra, drowned 36,380 people, and tore loose the chains of anchored ships in South America.

Colossal as it was, Krakatau's explosion was only a fraction as strong as the eruption at Thera. Eight square miles of Krakatau fell into the sea; Thera lost thirty-two square miles. Krakatau's crater was one fifth the size of Thera's. The ash that fell around Krakatau nowhere exceeded sixteen inches; the deposit on Thera was a hundred feet plus.

In 1956 an accidental discovery on the island aroused more interest among antiquaries. At the bottom of a mine shaft, Professor Angelos Galanopoulos of the Athens Seismological Institute found fire-blackened ruins of a stone house. Inside were pieces of charred wood and the teeth of a man and a woman. Radiocarbon analysis indicated that they died about 1400 B.C.—the approximate date assigned to the volcanic eruption.

So the proof began to look convincing: an island civilization had been shaken, abandoned, and submerged, much as Plato described it. Thera really could have been the center—or one of the key cities—of the fabled empire of Atlantis, since details of its death fitted Plato's story. Professor Galanopoulos propounded the Atlantis theory with deep conviction.

By 1967 enough people were interested to enable Marinatos (by then a professor emeritus and Inspector General of Antiquities for the Greek government) to take charge of systematic digging on the island. He kept at it for seven years, until he died in a fall at the site. He had estimated that a hundred years of excavation would be needed to uncover the whole city. Others carried on. Each season a house or two was uncovered, debris was sifted, tiny fragments of frescoes and pots were pieced together, streets were mapped, and structures were restored and strengthened.

"We had expected to find ruins of a prehistoric town—just foundations and fallen stones," a researcher said. "In most finds the ruins don't come up to your knees. Here we found not a ruin but a museum in three dimensions—every interior sealed under preserving ash or pumice."

The buildings weren't really intact, though. Many walls bulged outward from the force of the airblast when the volcano erupted. Frescoes were peppered with small holes, as from shotguns.

I prowled through ancient streets that the excavators had dug out. One large structure looked like a palace. In its storeroom I saw twenty man-sized vases, their insides coated with microscopic traces of old grain, oil, and wine. Elsewhere in the palace I saw a coppersmith's workshop; a sacrificial area where a blackened fireplace contained charred bones of lambs and birds; bronze roasting pans with flecks of what had been barley, flour, onions, buns, roasted snails, and sea urchins. There had been no time for dishwashing, evidently, after the Therans' last meal.

In one house I saw a commodious bathtub—but it was very short; the people were no more than five and a half feet tall. In another house was a rare find: layers of dark dust within the white volcanic ash. Researchers applied epoxy resin to harden it, and eventually drew forth a replica of a sizable basket of twigs and bark strips. Elsewhere was an impression in the dust, into which a master restorer had gently poured plaster. When the plaster hardened and the ash was scraped off, he had a plaster cast of a wooden bed so detailed that the thongs that had once bound the frame showed clearly. It was the first piece of wooden furniture recreated in an Aegean site.

I saw big wall paintings, some extending around a whole room. Bare-breasted women wore jeweled necklaces and eye makeup. Naked boys fought, wearing boxing gloves. Monkeys and antelopes cavorted; they were of species that now exist only in Africa, according to experts. A piece of one fresco showed a Negroid head. Did the empire of Atlantis stretch into Africa?

Apparently, Thera's city had taken the form of a circle, with the mountain at its center. Around this were rings of land and water, with bridges connecting the land rings, and canals big enough for ships connecting the water rings. The docks were on the outermost ring. It was a novel design—coinciding with Plato's description of the chief city of Atlantis: "fortified by a fence of alternate rings of sea and land, smaller and greater, one within another."

The harbor of Atlantis was "constantly crowded by merchant vessels and their passengers arriving from all quarters, whose vast numbers occasioned incessant shouting, clamor and general uproar day and night." Thera's harbor could have been like that, to judge from the dense neighborhoods, good-sized homes, and luxurious furnishings. The absence of gold and skeletons suggests that the ancient inhabitants had warning, as Plato said the Atlanteans had.

Professor Galanopolous said that Thera was part of the great Minoan civilization that spread through Crete and around the shores of the Aegean. All coastal cities were swept away by the wave from the dying Thera. But Knossos, where the legendary King Minos built his labyrinth for the Minotaur, was several miles inland on Crete, so it survived the tidal wave. It had been excavated.

I knew I had to see it.

# 4

# To Meet the Minotaur

Before I went there, I knew that the dead palace of Knossos sometimes had an odd effect on imaginative people. Leonard Cottrell, an eminent British archaeological writer, mentioned his feelings about it several times. In one book, *Lost Worlds,* he merely hinted:

> When one descends that shadowed Knossian staircase, with its colonnades opening onto a light-well, or when one stands in the dimly lit, frescoed rooms of state, one feels nearest to those remote people.

His disquiet showed more clearly in another book, *The Bull of Minos*. At one point he wrote:

> As I followed the curator to the Central Court, a curious, faint uneasiness began. . . . I am not a superstitious man; I have no belief in the super-

> natural. But I have to admit that the atmosphere of the Palace depressed me. It was—there is no other word for it—sinister.

Elsewhere in the same book he remarked, "There was something which had haunted me since I entered the Palace, a sense of doom, a smell of death."

John D. S. Pendlebury, after toiling for years to help Sir Arthur Evans exhume Knossos, wrote, "I defy anyone to enter the Throne Room without a strange thrill."

Sir Arthur himself, the hot-eyed little scholar who found the ruined palace and spent the equivalent of a million dollars reconstructing it, was first to notice strange sensations there. One warm moonlit night, unable to sleep, he wandered onto the five-flight grand staircase, which lay open to the sky with painted walls on either side. He felt something like ghosts there.

"It revives the remote past," he wrote of the stairway. "It was, indeed, my own lot to experience its strange power of imaginative suggestion." He went on:

> The whole place seemed to awake awhile to life and movement. Such was the force of the illusion that the Priest-King with his plumed lily crown, great ladies, long-stoled priests, and after them a retinue of elegant but sinewy youth—as if the Cup-Bearer and his fellows had stepped down from the walls—passed and repassed on the flights below.

I wondered if I would feel what Evans had felt. He had uncanny intuition. "One of Sir Arthur's greatest gifts was his capacity for visualizing," Piet de Jong, who worked with him for years, told a reporter. "He could tell, just by looking at a few broken stones, a fallen column and a few bits of fresco, exactly how the whole room or building originally looked. He'd get impatient if his architect couldn't see it just as quickly. Yet when the architect surveyed and measured, and studied all the architectural evidence, the fact is that Sir Arthur was nearly always right."

It was partly intuition that had led Evans to Knossos, I realized as I read about him. In 1893 he was rummaging through the curiosity dealers' trays in Shoe Lane in Athens when he noticed several tiny beads, some four-sided, some three-sided, drilled with a hole for thread. He was shortsighted, with almost microscopic eyesight when he studied things at close range. Scrutinizing the beads, he saw tiny squiggles that he thought might be hieroglyphics in a completely unknown language.

"Where are these from?" he asked the dealer, who replied that peasant women on Crete wore them as amulets. Certainly the peasants had not made these objects. On a hunch, he went to Crete, hoping to confirm a theory that prehistoric Greece had had a writing system.

From the day he landed, he felt a deep sense of the past. Homer had known and sung of this "rich and lovely land in the dark blue sea." It had ninety towns, Homer said, and "one of the ninety was a great city called Knossos . . . [where] King Minos ruled and enjoyed the friendship of almighty Zeus." Evans could see snow-capped Mount Ida, supposed birthplace of Zeus, crowning the mountainous skyline.

Evans roamed Crete, picking up more of the old beads inscribed with what he thought might be ancient Greek or Cretan writing. He wasn't yet much interested in Homeric myths; he wanted clay tablets or carved inscriptions.

His search led him to remote parts of the 160-mile-long island. Here and there he noticed traces of a once-mighty civilization. There had been great paved highways running from coast to coast. There had been aqueducts, altars, theaters, villas, seaports—all surprisingly different from the Greek and Roman styles.

Knossos, a mere village now, still existed a few miles inland from the port of Heraklion. Heinrich Schliemann, who found Troy and taught the world that Greek legends must be taken seriously after all, had been well aware of Homer's allusions to this and other places on the island. He planned to dig at Knossos, but quarreled with the owner of the land, and died soon after.

When Evans saw the piles of rubble and ruins that had fascinated Schliemann, he felt something nudge his own imagination.

He looked at massive walls and six-foot jars, uncovered by local trench-diggers. Could this have been a palace? Where there was a palace, there might be archives.

It was enough to make up his mind. He boldly announced that he represented a "Cretan Exploration Fund" (which then existed only in his mind) and wished to buy some land on the fund's behalf. Since he had inherited two fortunes, he could easily strike a bargain with the Turkish owner.

But then the Turkish government, which ruled Crete, refused to let him touch the land. When Crete was freed in 1900 he returned, bought the remainder of the site, wangled the new government's cooperation, and hired 150 workmen to help him excavate.

He was a man of demonic energy. It took him only nine weeks to make a sensational discovery. The ruins of supposedly mythical Knossos lay only a few feet underground; unlike most buried cities, it had not been built over later. The astonished Evans found himself looking at a sprawling, complex network of walls covering at least six acres.

The cellars contained miles of storerooms—great stone-built magazines with rows of smoke-blackened jars big enough to contain two men each, rather like those in which Ali Baba found the Forty Thieves. In these cellars Evans found what he sought: a hoard of almost two thousand clay tablets and stone seals, bearing symbols like those that had first set him on the trail. Evidently fires, gutting the palace, had accidentally baked and preserved the soft tablets (which the original scribes had used only for temporary notes). Evans confidently expected to decode the pictographs and scripts, but never succeeded. They turned out to be in three separate unknown languages, one of which is still impenetrable. I wondered if someday it would tell us the unknown history of the brilliant long-lived empire that Evans called Minoan.

Evans announced that he would need a year to

find everything of interest at the site. He underestimated. Forty-one years later he was still digging there. He went to Crete to decipher a system of writing, but he discovered a civilization.

Eventually he proved that Minoan ships were crossing seas as early as 4000 B.C., before any other known maritime power. Stretching back into the ancient days of mankind, before Zeus ruled in heaven, this civilization was at least as old as the pharaohs, and perhaps much older.

To strangers it must have looked benign and peaceful as well as grand. There were no fortifications on Crete. Not only Knossos was vast. The port of Heraklion, as the Greeks called it, was bigger than Athens. Across the island on the southern shore was Phaistos, also with a majestic unfortified palace. Two other palaces were later found elsewhere on Crete. Archaeologists began to realize that Cretan (Minoan) culture had been palace-centered.

It had overtones of evil. Because Knossos was built on the slope of a hill, it was five or more stories high in some parts. On upper levels were spacious chambers. In the dim depths underneath, what a contrast! Instead of splendid halls or sunny courtyards was an intricate coil of winding stairways and dead-end storagerooms and intersecting passages, bringing to mind the "labyrinth" in which Homer said King Minos kept the monstrous Minotaur.

So this much of the myth was fact. Minos did have a Maze.

Even on the upper floors, Minoan palaces were confusing, with many rooms and corridors. This labyrinthine design made them—to modern eyes, anyhow—places of terror. Probably these convolutions had a two-fold or three-fold purpose: to confuse intruders, to protect the center from intrusion, and possibly to confine someone or something.

The Maze became the Minoan trademark. We find heraldic versions of it on coins of Knossos for four centuries. Maze patterns decorated walls, found their way onto textiles, were inscribed on funerary urns and storage vats. What kind of people, I wondered, took such pride in bewildering and scaring the unwary?

And why were there no outer walls for defense? Why were there scarcely any signs of weapons or soldiers, until the very last years of the empire?

Control of the seas by a powerful navy could explain why Minoan lords felt secure against invasion from overseas. But what about attack by one lord against another? And was there no need for police protection, or compulsion, against the swarms of lower-class workers?

I recalled frightening tales about Crete in Greek mythology. The despot Minos had made a demand so wild and sinister that it might have emanated from a madhouse: he ordered Athens to send him fourteen youths and maidens each eight years (presumably to be given alive to the monster who lurked in the Maze). And Athens meekly complied.

And there was the tale of Daedalus, the peerless craftsman, the Maze Maker. He was a refugee from Athens because of a murder he committed there. Dazzling Minos with mechanical inventions and artistic novelties, he became a court favorite. But he tried to please everyone—including the king's wife Pasiphaë, whom the gods afflicted with a mad passion for a white bull. Daedalus contrived a lifelike dummy cow in which the queen crouched to receive the bull. The monstrous progeny of her lust was the bullheaded man, the Minotaur (literally the Bull of Minos) which the king hid in the Maze made by Daedalus.

Then came the strangest part of these legends. Enraged at Daedalus for conniving in Pasiphaë's amours, Minos locked him and his son in the Maze. It was there, the tales said, that Daedalus fashioned flying machines, one for himself and one for Icarus. They would rise out of Knossos like storks. Long afterward, the Greek Apollodorus wrote:

> Daedalus constructed wings for himself and his son, and enjoined his son neither to fly high, lest the glue should melt in the sun and the wings should drop off, nor to fly too near the sea, lest the pinions be detached by the damp.

> But the infatuated Icarus, disregarding his father's instructions, soared ever higher till, the glue melting, he fell into the sea called after him Icarian, and perished.

Empty-hearted, Daedalus flew on toward the chill north by tracks unknown. He alighted at Cumae, the first Greek colony in Italy. There he built a temple to Apollo. Then he journeyed to Sicily, and stirred that island to civilization by bringing it the artistic and industrial culture of the Minoans.

I wondered how much truth lay behind the legend of Daedalus's wings. I had only to examine bluffs overlooking the Pacific Ocean along the coast of southern California. With tools that Daedalus himself could have used, the young daredevils of today fashion hang-gliders. They are little more than two flimsy wings linked to each other by a bar. Perched on the bar, these modern Icaruses launch themselves into the updrafts, spinning up the faces of shoreline cliffs. Like surfers seeking a wave, the hang-gliders hope to encounter a spiraling air current that will lift them, unpowered, hundreds of feet into the air.

The Greeks never doubted that Daedalus had adventured in the sky. Virgil wrote of this legend. So did Ovid and Plutarch. Before them, the Greek poets Epimenides, Bacchylides, Cleidemus, and Philochorus mentioned the same story. As long as bards sang and children remembered, the tale of soaring Daedalus survived. In our time, the experience of Schliemann warned us to be skeptical even of our skepticism. Old myths and Bible stories have a way of being spurned by one generation of scholars, and laboriously confirmed by the next.

Delving further into legend, I found the Minoan myth lengthening and coiling back on itself like a labyrinth. The vengeful Minos went with his fleet in search of Daedalus, and, wrote Apollodorus, "in every country he searched he carried a spiral shell and promised a great reward to him who should pass a thread through the shell, believing that by that means he should discover Daedalus."

This was a cunning bait to catch an inventive fugitive. When Minos arrived at Sicily he showed the shell to the monarch there, Cocalus—who took it and promised to thread it. Daedalus was in hiding at his court, and Cocalus knew his talents. Daedalus could not resist the challenge. He found an elegant solution to the problem: he simply bored a hole in the spiral shell, fastened a thread to an ant, and enticed the ant to crawl into the shell and out the hole. But when Cocalus brought the threaded shell back to claim the reward, Minos knew Daedalus must be there, and demanded his surrender.

At this point the folk tales disagree. Some say that Daedalus slew Minos. Others say, with Apollodorus, "After his bath Minos was undone by the daughters of Cocalus." How? Only silence comes back. The great tyrant passed into darkness, done to death by means unknown. But his subjects still revered him. They said he reigned on in the underworld, passing final judgment on all the dead. What of his fleet? Wrecked on the coast of southern Italy, supposedly. But I wondered if it had sailed away to settle in faraway places.

Daedalus (the name means "cunning artificer") went on to other creations. He is said to have invented the saw, the ax, the gimlet, tongs, the plumb line, and the ball-and-socket joint. As his last feat he undertook to make a perfect honeycomb in gold.

What is more impossibly fragile to make in gold than a honeycomb? Diodorus Siculus, writing in the first century B.C., insisted that Daedalus really made one. But nobody who knew anything about metalwork believed this. Diodorus couldn't explain how it was done. For two thousand years the tale remained incredible.

Then in 1967 a British artist and sculptor, Michael Ayrton, conceived and described a method by which Daedalus could have cast the gold honeycomb. Ayrton himself made one. It was proof that Diodorus had told a true tale, and that Daedelus actually had lived.

It now appears that Minos was many men, not

one. The rulers at Knossos were always called Minos, as rulers of Egypt were called Pharaoh. According to Sir James Frazer, the great expert on magic and religion, every eight years Minos traditionally climbed to the cave on Mount Ida and gave an account of his kingship to his divine father Zeus. The tradition plainly implied that without this eight-year renewal he would have to forfeit the throne.

Why eight years? Because, Frazer said, only once in eight years does the full moon coincide with the shortest or longest day of the year. Minoans must have kept exact records of the rising and setting of the sun and the moon.

I surmised that this renewal of the king's power might have some secret connection with the octennial tribute of youths and maidens from Athens. This was another reason for suspecting that the Minotaur tale wasn't totally untrue.

But what happened to the youngsters when they arrived at Knossos? I couldn't credit the literal reality of a hybrid bull-man.

Frazer thought the youths might have been part of a terrible rite:

> Perhaps they were roasted alive in a bronze image of a bull, or of a bull-headed man, in order to renew the strength of the king. This at all events is suggested by the legend of Talos, a bronze man who clutched people and leaped with them into the fire.
>
> He is said to have been given by Zeus . . . to guard the island of Crete, which he patrolled thrice daily. According to one account he was a bull.
>
> Probably he was identical with the Minotaur, and stripped of mythical features was nothing but a bronze image. Human victims may have been sacrificed to the idol by being roasted in its hollow body.

Talos? The Greeks said he was a giant of brass who kept strangers off Crete by throwing huge rocks at approaching ships. Or he made himself red-hot and burned trespassers to death in his embrace.

If people believed this, it could account for the absence of fortifications on the island. No one would dare approach. But Talos sent my trail winding back on itself again. Some legends said he was nephew to Daedalus; others say that he was the great engineer's apprentice.

Well, whatever the truth of the tales, Minos and Talos and the Minotaur in the Maze made Crete sound terribly uninviting to strangers. All the more reason I should go and see it, I thought.

# 5

# Into the Maze

The seas around the legend-haunted island were gray-blue almost to blackness. Crete stretched clear across the horizon long before my motor launch reached it. As we drew nearer, the view was harsh and spectacular, fit only for wild goats and bandits, today as in antiquity. Once Crete was famed for its oaks and cypresses, olives and vines, and abundant springs. But now the springs are dry, and Crete is mostly barren because of Christian and Saracen mismanagement during and after the Middle Ages.

Even at its greenest, Crete must have looked cruel to those in the tribute-ships approaching the capital, because they would see only the high shores—huge wrinkled yellow cliffs hiding the land beyond. Where the cliffs opened to a river mouth, they would sail into the big harbor at Heraklion (or Amnistos, as the Minoans seem to have called it, or Candia, as it is called in most of today's travel guides) and see houses like rows of towers, three or four stories high. The waterfront would be crowded with Minoans, small and brown and quick-eyed, watching to see the captives brought ashore.

In the Minoans' heyday, the route to Knossos was a stone highway for chariots and carts. But earthquakes and tidal waves and storms of brimstone from Thera long ago obliterated the pavement. Today there is only a rough dirt road.

I drove along it, through the port and up into a winding steep-sided valley. This too would have seemed forbidding to Theseus and other captives. But their trip was short, for the road rose and fell until, only four miles inland, it came out on a little plain with a range of stark rocky mountains beyond.

Even then, almost at their destination, captives may not have seen Knossos. I didn't, at first.

The great palace lay in a hollow, half hidden by trees and slopes. Only the northern side, the way to the sea, was open. When we got there I was still musing about why this mountainous island became the center of an empire. Other great civilizations of about the same time—Egypt, Mesopotamia, the Indus Valley—grew up along fertile river valleys. But Crete had no large rivers, and few plains. How could a highly distinctive culture arise here and flourish for two thousand years?

I forgot this riddle when I noticed, sharp against the hard blue Cretan sky, a mighty pair of sculpted horns like those of a gigantic bull. They reared over the highest roof edge of the Palace of Minos.

Such insolent horns, which Evans called horns of consecration, stood atop many Minoan palaces, I remembered reading. Minoan religion seemed to adore the bull; its horns were the only substitute for the aspiring steeples and domes in most religious centers of other empires. The roofs of Knossos were flat, without even watchtowers or battlements.

I walked up a paved ramp into a courtyard, and saw a fresco of a great red bull charging across a wall. Beyond the threshold, past low walls and smooth pavement and crimson columns (tapering downward, strangely), I made a turn and was inside the palace.

This was no open yard of knee-high ruins or bare walls. Sir Arthur Evans had not only tunneled out and cleared, he had rebuilt and repainted and redecorated. The Minoans had built with only limestone and gypsum, and used wooden beams and posts, which tended to rot eventually. Sir Arthur substituted reinforced concrete, overlaid with wood or coated to resemble the original. He was determined that Knossos should rise again in a form that would not only satisfy archaeologists but also give unschooled visitors a vivid impression of what the palace had been. So he restored walls, floors, ceilings, porticoes, and pillars. He reconstructed decorations by piecing together whatever was found, and using his imagination to fill in the rest. Purists objected to his guesswork but had to admit that the rebuilt palace fitted every available clue.

I wandered across sunny courtyards, up and down stairways, through echoing corridors, along colonnades barred with shadows, and in and out of magnificent apartments till I couldn't tell east from west. I stopped many times to admire frescoes. There was nothing grim about Minoan artwork; everything was bright and full of movement, with cheerful subjects.

There were sportive fishes, swooping birds, children gathering flowers, crowds of classic-featured chattering ladies with painted lips and naked breasts, aglitter with ornaments, and graceful half-nude men with slim waists, black braided hair, and jeweled bracelets and bangles. There was a young prince in a gaudy feather headdress (like an Aztec?) with lilies, a symbol of royalty, beside him.

Everywhere I felt the strangeness of Knossos. We were only a few hundred miles from Egypt, to which the Minoans had sailed for two thousand years. Yet, there was nothing Egyptian—or Grecian—in the architecture, or in the faces or dress of these people. Who were they? Where had they come from? Where had they gone?

Only one or two levels of the huge edifice had been rebuilt. Above had once been floor upon floor. Light wells brought in sunshine and air. The hydraulic system was far beyond anything else of its kind in antiquity. This was a plumbers' paradise, as Cottrell called it. Great stone channels led the water from the roof through shafts to baths and toilets, and led off the waste in terra-cotta pipes that were themselves ventilated by air shafts and made accessible by roomy manholes.

Rooms of state were approached by majestic shallow staircases. We know what sort of rooms these were, through the almost miraculous preservation of the queen's private quarters on one side of a great central court, and a throne room on the other.

The queen's suite was a place seemingly not of stone and wood but of light and color. The walls glowed with frescoes of dolphins leaping on an eggshell-blue sea. The columns writhed with bright painted curlicues. Everything shone: designs on the ceiling, mosaics on the floor. All around me, blues and greens and yellows shimmered as if I stood inside a prism. Only the low seats around the walls were subdued.

As for the Room of the Throne, it made me slightly nervous, as it did Pendlebury. I went in through a low-ceilinged anteroom, opened a wooden door, and stood in the wide dim room of the mysterious kings. Against the wall, in its original place, rose the oldest throne in Europe—stark and simple, but skillfully carved, with rounded seat and high curved back. On either side were guardian griffins. They were painted on a blue field of lilies, but they were ugly lionlike creatures with vulture heads. Along the walls were stone benches where priests had sat watching. The floor was hard glazed earth.

To those who had revered Minos, the room could have seemed like a cathedral chapter house. But to me it spoke of dark gods and the ghost waiting for the ferry on the sighing shore. I felt glad to stride out into the sparkling Cretan sunshine.

Imagine to yourself all the grandest mansions you ever saw, set beside each other and piled on one another. That would be a little house beside the Palace of Minos. This was a town within a palace. Knossos housed hundreds of people night and day. The entire lower part of its western side was used for official quarters, teeming with clerks and civil servants and priests (but no armed guards, apparently). This building housed not only residences and offices but also cult centers, theaters, anterooms, meeting halls, washrooms, workshops, storerooms, and kitchens in one human beehive. Its cellars were a far-reaching dark warren of passages and vaults.

The place was somehow dreadful in its size and grandeur. Everywhere I saw reproductions of the fearsome sacred bulls. And the double ax, or its emblems, were also common. Did you know that *labrys*, from which we derive "labyrinth," is a non-Greek word picked up from some forgotten language? It means a double-edged ax. This ax was as omnipresent in Cretan religion as the cross is in Christianity.

The bull, the ax, the maze: what sinister fetishes for a seemingly sunny civilization! Knossos, to me, was a palace built on fear—such overpowering fear that its rulers felt totally secure; such fear that vassals like King Aegeus gave up the flower of their youth when no compulsion was visible.

The first Cretan palaces arose quite suddenly, scholars believe. No one has satisfactorily explained why or how. Whoever built these structures commanded great resources in materials and manpower, and had access to ideas and goods from Egypt, Syria, and even Babylonia.

The Minoans sent their trading ships far and wide. To what extent they established colonies is uncertain, but Thucydides, that most reliable of ancient historians, wrote, "The first person known to us by tradition as having established a navy is Minos. He made himself master of what is now called the Hellenic sea, and ruled over the Cyclades, into most of which he sent the first colonies." If this is so, those colonies are gone without trace.

Where did this civilization spring from? Evans sank test pits, and proved that there had been continuous settlement at Knossos from about 3000 B.C. down to about 1150 B.C. Before the third millennium, all the way back to the cavemen, there is only conjecture, but various clues suggest that groups of wanderers voyaged to Crete from Spain and from Asia Minor.

By the twentieth century B.C. a giant sea empire had spread out from Knossos. Its ships sailed to the Levant and the Nile delta, to Rhodes, Cyprus, Sicily, the Bay of Naples, Marseilles, and the coast of Spain. Its seafarers could not have been warriors, since weapons appear only very late in the development of Minoan culture.

This peaceful empire put down piracy throughout the Aegean and the Mediterranean—apparently without warships. Everyone seems to have feared and obeyed them, perhaps because they were the only men who dared to venture far from land. Did the rest of the known world think they were gods?

There is a theory that legends of Atlantis were garbled descriptions of Minoan Crete. Somewhere around 1400 B.C., when the empire was at a peak of power and prosperity, disaster came suddenly, as it supposedly did to Atlantis. The giant waves racing out from Thera engulfed Minoan cities on the coasts—but not Knossos, since it was inland and on higher ground. The palace of Knossos was leveled at least once by an earthquake, only to be rebuilt more grandly. It survived at least a half century after Thera's destruction.

Then it too was destroyed. At Knossos and at other sites on Crete are clear signs of fire: charred beams and pillars, blackened stone, clay tablets baked solid. There had been sudden panic. In one room, the excavators found a block of purple Spartan basalt half sawed through, as if abandoned in haste. In the throne room were evidences of an unfinished religious ceremony.

Evans thought an earthquake started the fire. Pendlebury, his younger assistant, thought Knossos was attacked and looted, probably by raiders from mainland Greece.

My own amateur hunch was that Pendlebury was right. After all, Knossos recovered from earlier disasters caused by earthquakes, but this time it did not. Also, in modern cities with gas mains and power lines, earthquakes often start bad fires, but this wasn't necessarily true in the ancient world. Many Minoan cities apparently burned as if put to the torch. And nothing of value was found in them (except at Zakros, which was packed in volcanic ash). Invaders would have carried off the missing valuables. So I think someone discovered that Crete was rotten-ripe for plucking. When they came, whoever they were, they may merely have hastened an inevitable doom.

Knossos was never rebuilt, although squatters occupied the ruins for a long time. But where did the Minoans (or Atlanteans?) go when fleeing their palaces? The end of their empire is a mystery as dark as the mystery of Minoan script. The Minoans, like the Etruscans, suffer from having their history written by others. Even their walls show no pictures of historic events.

Their pictures are purely decorative or entertaining—such as the famous paintings of youths performing perilous acrobatics on the horns of bulls. Such stunts would be impossible, according to modern matadors and rodeo stars.

No similar "bull dance" paintings have been found outside Crete. But there are inklings that some islanders may have gone to Asia Minor and fathered the brutal Philistines, who warred on Hebrews. Others probably sailed elsewhere. Herodotus and Strabo say that Cretans founded Troy. Homer says that a grandson of Minos, Idomenus, led one of the famous contingents against Troy under Agamemnon. A scattering of finds that suggest Minoan mazes have turned up along the edges of Europe—and of America.

A maze is carved on a very old stone in Holywood, in northern Ireland. A maze decorates an Etruscan vase. There are large stone chambers surrounded by winding stone passages, the whole covered by massive roof slabs, along the Atlantic coasts in Spain and Portugal, northwestern France, western England, the western isles of Scotland and the Orkneys, northern Germany and Denmark, and southern Norway and Sweden.

The resemblance among these, scattered along five thousand miles of coast within a span of at most two hundred years, is so close that no expert doubts that they are related to one another. But are they Minoan? No one can say, yet.

Could Minoans—refugees from a fallen civilization—have sailed all the way to prehistoric America? About two hundred small ancient sites have recently been dug up in New England. They contain stone sacrificial tables and bowls similar to some at the ritual chambers of Knossos. They are certainly not Viking or Celtic or Mayan. They might be Minoan.

At Mystery Hill, New Hampshire, there is a stone labyrinth. On its walls are inscriptions that, according to Harvard epigrapher Barry Fell and others, resemble Minoan hieroglyphs. If they are, then America was discovered by Europeans more than three thousand years before Columbus sailed, more than twenty-five centuries before the Vikings came.

My visit to Mystery Hill had convinced me that native Americans, American Indians, had not created the settlement. Where most tribes built shelter of wood and animal skins, Mystery Hill is made of piled rock, like the palaces on Crete. Maze-like in structure, an oracle chamber dominates one part of the Mystery Hill construction much the same as the chamber on Crete.

The notion seems provable that the first visitors to America from the east were the roaming Phoenicians, not the Vikings, or the explorers of England, Holland, Spain, Portugal and Italy. I found one other tantalizing bit of evidence.

Ingrid Beckman, a young psychic, recently visited Mystery Hill knowing nothing about archaeologists' theories. She noticed emanations that, she thought, came from very far back in prehistory. They gave her nightmarish thoughts of beasts and axes. Another medium, Ethel Meyers, got impressions of three different races at the site—including one race that flew.

Elsewhere are other unexplained finds that might be links to the Minoans. On a rock at Lake Assawompsett, Massachusetts, is a carving of a ship—rather like the Minoan ships, with high bow and stern and one square sail on a central mast.

There is a stone near Fort Benning, Georgia, with

markings that could be Minoan. At two places in Brazil, near the coast, are stones bearing inscriptions in a similar unreadable language.

If Minoans got to America, they probably died in lonely destitution. After the luxury of their palaces and the warmth of Crete, prehistoric North America would have been rigorous indeed. Any Minoans who were here left no permanent traces, with the possible exception of those strange stone relics.

So there was no way I could follow their faint trail any farther into the New World. But there were other sea trails I wanted to follow farther: the trails of certain Homeric heroes in the Aegean Sea.

Hercules, for example. Was the Cretan port of Heraklion named for him? Legend said that Minos sent for him to dispose of the white bull that had impregnated Queen Pasiphaë and run loose afterward. Hercules came, captured the bull, and bore it off to Tiryns, which might have been a Minoan colony, in Greece's southern peninsula.

And what of Odysseus, the Cunning One, as Homer called him? He sometimes claimed to be a grandson of Minos.

And where did Theseus go? Legend said he fled from Knossos with Minos's daughter Ariadne. On the isle of Naxos he married her, as he had promised—but while she slept he and his Athenian shipmates sailed away. She stayed on at Naxos to become the wife of jolly Bacchus, who posthumously ascended into the pantheon as god of pleasure.

Meanwhile, Theseus went home and was crowned king of Athens. He sent for and married the Minoan princess Phaedra. (Minos lay dead in Sicily long since.) Then Theseus's luck forsook him. Phaedra hanged herself. Their son was killed by a bull. Theseus went off to seek centaurs (and lovely women) in the mountains of Thessaly, but got into some scrape from which his kinsman Hercules rescued him. At the isle of Skyros he fell off a high rock—perhaps through his host's treachery—and drowned in the sea. His younger son Akamas, the half-Minoan, succeeded to the throne and led the Athenians into the confederacy that made war on Troy.

Since so many other Greek legends turned out to have a factual basis, might there not be some truth in these too?

When you begin by pursuing a myth as potent as the labyrinth, you follow the winding ways wherever they lead. Finding your way out only takes you deeper in. Very well. I would roam the Aegean, tracking Theseus and Hercules and the dreaded Minos, until I reached the great ruined citadel of Troy.

# 6

# What the Cyclopes Left

As I put to sea, myths of the Aegean wove around my imagination like a dark garland. I was back in the pagan world where Jason's *Argo* fought the heaving waves in quest of the Golden Fleece, where Hercules labored, where Odysseus outwitted sirens and Cyclopes, where gods feasted overhead while Troy at their feet clanged with the conflict of arms.

Islands glowed green and violet in the distance. They were what fascinated and drew men into the Aegean, those shadowed hills that rose in a haze of opal light and seemed to float weightlessly upon the water. At dusk the colors died, sinking in the rising mist as if Father Poseidon were drawing them under the waves to sleep. There were few sights lovelier on earth. Sailing the Aegean, I thought I understood why men who had lived near those coasts and islands of mystery and enchantment had come to love them almost more than life, and had thought exile worse than death.

And I also understood, that night, why voyagers on the Aegean were glad that they were seldom out of sight of land. I heard the whistle of a rising gale. It was a south wind, which throughout the ages had closed Cretan waters to ships from the north. The gusts came hard and often, speeding our ship along, for we were heading northwest toward the land nearest to Crete: Peloponnesus.

By the bright moon I saw white cloud masses scud off toward ancient pirate camps among the Cyclades. (The Minoan empire wiped out piracy. But after the last Minos died, sea rovers made many flying raids along the coast, until Theseus temporarily put them down again.) The gale blew higher, and our running lights threw shadows that flitted and pitched and swooped, as if creatures of the dark had come to play. It was a night when chimeras and harpies and gorgons might be abroad, when perhaps the old gods stirred in their caves and strode over the sea.

Nearing Cape Malea, the peninsula's southernmost tip, we crossed Odysseus's sea trail. As he returned from the Trojan War, he tried merely to sail home to Ithaca on the west side of the peninsula, but his battered ship was blown like a runaway chariot past the cape, into the unknown western Mediterranean, and down toward the Libyan coast, where he met the lotus eaters. And so he went, winding through a labyrinth, seeking a home that faded farther from him, fated not to reach Ithaca until ten years later.

Homer told a lot about winds, currents, number of days at sea, and land seen. But he himself could not have sailed much. In his time—around 900 or 800 B.C.—Greeks were just emerging from a "dark age" of four centuries in which they did little traveling.

Nevertheless, Homer wrote that an offshore wind propelled Odysseus past Cape Malea and Cape Matapan. This rang true. Many centuries later, just such a wind drove St. Paul helplessly from Crete to shipwreck on Malta. And in my own journeyings I had heard Greek sailors growl about the "Greco," or "Greek wind," that often prevented them from skirting the southern Greek headlands.

But a different wind was blowing today—a norther, pushing us along. This was the wind that perversely bottled up 1,186 Greek ships assembled in the port of Aulis, ready to sail for Troy. Only when Agamemnon took a soothsayer's advice and sacrificed his own daughter on an altar—thus fulfilling a curse on his family—did the ill wind abate. How often, I wondered, had contrary winds shaped the fates of ancient Greeks?

In the morning we skimmed up the eastern Peloponnesian coast. Spray sang from the bow, and dolphins played around us like puppies, while I admired the purple land on our port side. Peloponnesus is the southernmost quarter of the Greek mainland. Its name, which means "Pelops' Isle" (although it isn't really an island) commemorated a daring wanderer who won a throne there.

I had heard the story of Pelops. He came from Asia Minor to seek the hand of a certain Greek princess—a perilous quest, because the king, who had been warned in a prophecy that his son-in-law would kill him, sought to prevent his daughter's marriage by challenging any suitor to a chariot race. The suitors had always lost, and their penalty was death.

But Pelops won, married the princess, and himself became king. He had bribed a groom to tamper with the royal chariot: the wheels flew off during the race, and the king was killed. When the groom demanded his reward—half of the kingdom and one night in the arms of the princess—Pelops drowned him. As he sank, the man put a curse on Pelops and all his breed.

The curse hung on for four generations. Pelops and his children came to bad ends. His grandsons Menelaus and Agamemnon ruled Sparta and Mycenae respectively, but both had faithless wives. Menelaus's beautiful wife, Helen (whose "face launched a thousand ships"), ran off to Troy with a lover, and Agamemnon mobilized an expedition to fetch her back, thus starting the siege of Troy. When Agamemnon at last came triumphantly home, his own wife and her paramour caught him unarmed and cut him to pieces. The cycle of doom took one more turn. Agamemnon's son Orestes killed the treacherous pair, then went mad. The Furies (underworld demons who avenged spilled family blood) followed him in a swarm all over the Aegean.

To see the place where this bloodstained family had lived out its fate, I went ashore—not from morbid curiosity, but because fabled "Mycenae, rich in gold," as Homer described it centuries after its fall, might have been a refuge for Minoans from Crete. The trip would have been a short one for them.

I landed at Argos, the natural terminus for sailing from Crete. I drove up into mountains and across the peaceful Argive plain—and suddenly beetling cliffs thrust up dead ahead. Anyone who has read of the long-ago happenings here would have felt uneasy. The cliffs were wild, naked, menacing, the scene of appalling deeds.

One more turn, then the remnants of a city spread around me.

A stone gateway about eighteen feet high opened into the hillside. I knew it as the entrance to the supposed tomb of Agamemnon. Standing in the giant doorway, I peered up at its stone crosspiece, which weighed 240,000 pounds by archaeologists' estimates. It was about thirty feet long and sixteen feet wide and more than three feet thick. Carved from a single piece of limestone, the crosspiece was a larger building unit than any used in Egyptian pyramids. Yet somehow these unknown Mycenaeans had maneuvered it onto the stone uprights without cranes or jacks, and fitted it neatly into place, where it stayed for three thousand years.

Next to Agamemnon, the hero of this place was Heinrich Schliemann, the self-taught German archaeologist. His father brought him up on Homer's stories of the siege of Troy and the wanderings of Odysseus. Little Heinrich naïvely believed every word. At the age of eight he announced his intention of devoting his life to the rediscovery of the lost cities of Troy and Mycenae. And he did.

He learned twelve languages including both ancient and modern Greek, married a Greek woman, named his son Agamemnon, and called a servant Pelops. When he had amassed enough money and knowledge, he went to a hill on the eastern edge of the Aegean Sea, where he dug and found Troy; then up into Peloponnesus, where he uncovered the royal Mycenaean graves with their trappings of gold leaf, swords, goblets, and gold death masks. Thus he proved Homer's worth as a historian.

But it took time. The world of academe doubted Schliemann's reports. The museums of Europe long refused to accept as genuine the relics he found. Few scholars saw any likelihood that there really had been a Troy, an Agamemnon, or any of the other places and people described in Greek myths.

While professional archaeologists believed that the Homeric poems were merely works of fiction, they were impressed by the ten-volume travel guide of Pausanias, who toured Greece about 160 A.D. and wrote of what he saw. He visited Mycenae when it was already a ruin, but there was no reason to doubt that he was shown tombs that local tradition had ascribed to Agamemnon and the rest of the accursed family. Pausanias wrote that the treacherous queen and her lover "were buried a little outside the wall, for they were not deemed worthy of burial within it, where Agamemnon lies and those who were murdered with him."

To the experts of Schliemann's day, "the wall" meant some small long-vanished wall enclosing a large area around the city of Mycenae. But Schliemann had found Troy by depending on Homer. This time he staked his claim on the full text of Pausanias, pointing out:

> That he had solely in view the walls of the Citadel, he shows by saying that in the wall is the Lion's Gate. . . . There cannot be any doubt that he had solely in view the huge Cyclopean walls he saw, and not those which he did not see. . . . He could not see the wall of the lower city because it had been originally very thin, and had been demolished 638 years before his time.

Schliemann kept digging and found tombs holding nineteen skeletons literally laden with gold. But more remarkable than the wealth was the artistry of the goldwork, which could have been done only by highly skilled craftsmen in a long-established civilization.

In 1876 the educated world followed Schliemann's work at Mycenae as breathlessly as a later generation would follow Howard Carter's excavations at Tutankhamen's tomb. By then scholars admitted that the German dilettante had a strong case, because (1) treasures in the graves corresponded to items described by Homer; (2) Homer had mentioned big body shields for which there was no parallel in classical times, or even in Homer's own period—yet in the tombs there were tiny sketches of men holding just such shields, on gold-inlaid dagger blades and gold signet rings; (3) Homer mentioned a helmet covered with boars' tusks, and in one tomb were sixty boars' teeth, all ground flat and pierced as if to fasten them to something—like a helmet.

Turning from the gaping graves, I wandered around the walls of Agamemnon's fortress. They were built of unhewn, unmortared blocks "so large that a pair of mules could not stir the smallest," as Pausanias wrote. A hundred generations of villagers had tried to dislodge the stones for their own use, yet large parts of the walls still survived, to attest to the immemorial cheapness of labor and uneasiness of kings.

The Mycenaeans, whoever they were, had been spectacular builders. These mighty ramparts were thirty feet thick in some places. The awed natives called the walls Cyclopean, believing that only the legendary one-eyed giants known as Cyclopes, who dwelled in mountain caves and were portrayed in Greek vase paintings, could have built them. (Today we surmise that the Cyclopes worked in quarries, and attached lanterns—the single glaring eyes—to their foreheads to give them light underground.)

I walked around the outside, counting paces, and found that the citadel was more than half a mile in circumference. Because of its strategic location, Schliemann had had no difficulty finding it. It commanded both the broad plain and the pass that led to Corinth and the western sea. When Schliemann arrived, the high walls were still half exposed, although the dust of thousands of years covered most of the ruins, and sheep grazed where kings had ruled.

As Schliemann and his successors pieced together clues, they decided that several villages must have been clustered in and around the citadel, housing a busy population of peasants, merchants, artisans, and soldiers. The king in his hilltop palace commanded a class of landholders whose estates were tilled by tenants or slaves. They sent quotas of horses, chariots, armor, and sheep to the king, and their tenants provided hides, honey, and wheat.

Within the palace, the scribal bureaucracy evidently kept tabs on a complex society. There were bronzesmiths and bowmakers, shepherds and weavers, fullers, unguent boilers, painters.

The great building itself seemed almost as intricate as those on Crete. It had been decorated mostly in the Minoan manner. I walked through dozens of ruined rooms, now open to the sky and choked with weeds. Here once were painted floors, columned porticoes, grand stairways, and frescoed walls. The frescoes that remained showed that Mycenaean ladies followed the opulent fashions of the women of Knossos. Art found in some graves was unmistakably Minoan.

Either an influx from Crete or contact with it stimulated Mycenae to become more refined if not less brutal. Nobody knows how the Mycenaean civilization began or where it came from. Like most, it probably arose from an interplay of migrant breeds and heritages. If the Mycenaeans' ancestors were Minoans, they themselves became something quite different. They were taller and broader, and often bearded. (Minoan men were always clean-shaven.) They used bronze swords and armor, and gloried in deeds of hunting and war. Their fondness for hunting got into Greek myths; one of the labors of Hercules was to capture a wild boar, which he carried to the marketplace at Mycenae.

The last few lords of Mycenae had Cretan artists

engrave for them, on vases and rings, a proud record of feats of banditry. Mycenae was well placed for its citizens to plunder travelers on the higher road from the Gulf of Argolis to the Isthmus of Corinth, and to set out occasionally on raids by land or by sea. So it grew rich on warfare, piracy, and trade.

As it reclaimed trade routes of the Cretan sea empire, its great shadow spread across seas and coastlines. A noted British archaeologist, Geoffrey Bibby, wrote of the Minoan and Mycenaean seafarers:

> Apparently, from about the middle of the Third Millennium to about the middle of the Second Millennium B.C., a very large area of the world was continuously known and traversed. The civilized portion was small, comprising little more than Greece, Crete and Asia Minor, Egypt and Palestine, Syria and Mesopotamia. But from this circumscribed area traders, missionaries, and perhaps even casual tourists went out, journeying over incredible distances, and doing this so habitually that there can be no doubt that the traffic was regular, safe—and profitable.
>
> And yet it ended. In the course of a few centuries, most of the world reverted to a subsistence economy, the trade routes dead and forgotten.

Beginning about 1400 B.C., when Minoans were refugees and landlubbers, Mycenae was the capital of a new empire. Its red sails with their guarding lions were known along the wharves of Egypt, Syria, and Palestine, as well as on the Danube and in the Bay of Naples. Schliemann didn't suspect this, even though he opened tombs containing ostrich eggs from Nubia, lapis lazuli from Mesopotamia, ivory from Syria, silver from Spain and Anatolia, amber from the Baltic, and scarabs and blue glass from Egypt. He assumed that these rare treasures had been brought in by visiting traders: How could a mountain people like the Mycenaeans so suddenly become a sea power?

At that time Schliemann knew nothing of the collection of Mycenaean pottery found later in the buried chambers of Egypt's Thutmose III. Nor did he know of the fine Mycenaean earthenware to be found in Cyprus, Palestine, Sicily, Malta, Sardinia, and Spain.

Historians now call the fourteenth and thirteenth centuries B.C. the Mycenaean age. By 1300 B.C. Mycenae was far richer than any other city in Europe. In size, in the splendor of her artworks, and in the impregnable location of her fortress-palace Mycenae had no rival—except perhaps nearby Tiryns, one of her numerous vassal states. Mycenae's last king was called "lord of all Argos and many islands" by Homer, who said that Agamemnon alone contributed no less than a hundred ships to the fleet that sailed against Troy.

One morning in 1190 B.C. or thereabout, Agamemnon and his men marched out through their proud Gate of Lions for their last campaign. I felt the wind blowing in from the sea as it had then, whipping the horsehair plumes on the helmets of the warriors. I imagined their women and children watching as they filed down the winding valley on the four-hour march to their ships.

I too went out through the Gate of Lions, and glanced up at the two royal beasts, now worn and headless, who stood guard over a long-gone grandeur. Mycenae's riddle lay not in its end but its beginning, long before Pelops—perhaps as early as 3000 B.C. —and I found no clue to that among the silent stones.

I was thinking of Greek myths again. Myth said, and Pausanias repeated, that the original builder of Mycenae was Perseus the gorgon slayer. His name meant "destroyer," and he was the forebear of the Persians. After founding Mycenae (which he named for a mushroom he found growing there), he supposedly moved to the older town nearby, Tiryns, and ruled there with an "Ethiopian princess" as his queen. According to some stories, Hercules was their great-grandson—he was born in Tiryns and was a longtime intermittent resident, so he was often called "the Tirynthian."

All this reminded me of something I had copied from the revised edition of the *Cambridge Ancient History:*

> Perseus . . . Hercules . . . Minos, Theseus, Jason . . . it has been common in modern times to regard these and other heroes of this age as purely mythical.
>
> The later Greeks, in criticizing the records of their past, had no doubt that they were historical persons who actually ruled in Argos and other kingdoms; and after a period of extreme skepticism many modern critics have begun to revert to the Greek view as that which explains the evidence most satisfactorily.
>
> The heroes of the tales, like the geographical scenes in which they moved, were real.

Certainly Tiryns of the Great Walls, as Homer called it, was real. Its massive ruins are only ten miles south of Mycenae. I went to them through peaceful fields of corn and wheat.

On a hill five miles east of Argos and one mile north of the sea, the ruins of the old fortress sleep like a giant land tortoise, long and low and gray, with a rocky knob at the head. I could see why seven Cyclopes were said to have built it. The walls were more than fifty feet thick at some places, and their corners were so neat that Pausanias said they bore comparison with Egypt's pyramids. The ponderous granite blocks—up to ten feet long by three feet in breadth and depth—were not square-cut, but were rough-hewn and fitted together with pebbles and clay, like those at Mycenae.

Some walls contained long galleries inside, vaulted and arched, opening onto the outside through black holes like gun ports. Probably archers had stood there. The galleries themselves must have led to armories, storerooms, and guard chambers and towers.

Archaeologists before Schliemann thought these ruins were of an unknown medieval castle (of which Greece had none, of course). But Greek legend said the walls were built two centuries before the Trojan War. Even then the town itself was older than Mycenae, which copied its style. In fact, modern X-rays show remains of an immense circular building at Tiryns that probably dates back five thousand years, but they are under the huge ruins of the later palace, so they can't be explored.

Although it seemed dwarfed by those gigantic surrounding walls, the palace was big. There in the building where Perseus's royal line had lived I was again reminded of Knossos.

A broad paved court was bound by colonnades. Around it were pillared walls and chambers, a thirteen-hundred-square-foot hall of state with a painted stone floor, a stately porch where royal servants slept, a throne room and antechamber, even a bath where Homer's heroes were bathed and anointed. Surrounding this central complex was a Minoan medley of workshops, storerooms, and stables.

Dolphins on blue squares in the floor resembled those in the queen's suite at Knossos. Big vases were richly decorated in a style I had seen in Crete. Along the main hall I saw an alabaster frieze in which the spirals were picked out in blue glass paste—another technique imported by the Minoans, or perhaps stolen from them.

I was puzzled by these similarities among Knossos, Mycenae, and Tiryns—as well as by the differences between Knossos and the latter two. Were these two mainland cities ruled from Knossos at one time? Or were they decorated by refugees, or captives?

Anyhow, there was no doubt that Tiryns had been a sort of satellite of Mycenae. Agamemnon and his forefathers were so powerful that they tolerated this other city nearby, and probably collected tribute from it. At Troy, the warlord of Tiryns (Diomedes) served under the commander in chief, Agamemnon. And after the war, Tiryns suffered the same fate as Mycenae. Its masonry was black from a great fire.

But now I was intent on the trails of young Theseus, his kinsman Hercules, and other figures of myth. Theseus probably never saw Tiryns. Hercules left it to sail with Jason in search of the Fleece.

I took ship again, to go after them.

# 7

# A Blind Man's Secrets

Cruising east through the Cyclades, I saw the purple profile of Naxos, my next stop.

This was the isle where young Theseus deserted his sleeping bride, Ariadne, who had helped him escape from her father, King Minos.

I wondered if Theseus had been a womanizer and a braggart. However, some scholars suggested that he forsook Ariadne because he discovered that she was a secret devotee of Bacchus, the youngest god, who gave wine to man. In *The Greek Way,* Edith Hamilton wrote of this festive but ill-fated god: "His death was terrible: he was torn to pieces. . . . He was always brought back to life; he died and rose again."

His death and resurrection was, supposedly, the excuse for a wild ritual that went back to a pre-Greek religion and forward to various modern cults in America, Africa, and elsewhere. In spring, when the grapes were blooming, women in this secret sorority took dark roads into the hills to meet their reborn god. For two days they drank, lurching in processions led by maenads, or madwomen. Their frenzied climax was to pull a living man to pieces, then drink his blood and eat his flesh in a sacred communion whereby, they thought, Bacchus entered them and possessed their souls.

The strangest part of the Ariadne story was that she married Bacchus on Naxos after Theseus left. Did this second husband die and rise again? If not, who was the man torn apart in the ritual?

Sir James Frazer suggested that perhaps it wasn't a man but a bull. Ariadne had reasons to feel strongly about bulls.

Another possibility, posed by Robert Graves, a noted writer on classical myths, was that the maenads' alleged custom of tearing off their victim's head might refer allegorically to tearing off and eating the heads of sacred mushrooms. In any case, if Theseus heard that Ariadne took part in the rite, I could see why he stole away. I sailed away too—after sampling the white wine for which Naxos is still noted.

Bacchus, I was told, was embodied in the pine tree. Worshipers slashed the trunk, cupped the flowing resin, and added it to wine in their casks. The result was Greece's famous resinated wine—bitterish, aromatic, like pine sap. Another story said that the later Athenians, scheming to save their wine during the Persian invasions by making it repellent to the intruders, doctored the storage jars with pine resin. The Persians found the mixture unpotable, as planned. But the Greeks tasted it afterward—and have been drinking *retsina,* with its taste like turpentine, ever since.

From Naxos, Theseus sailed home to Athens. I felt as though he pulled me after him, down the invisible passages of my own maze. My motor launch hugged the islands along the way, as had Theseus's ship. He sailed without compass or chart, and feared storms on the open sea.

Yet the worst waters to be crossed lay close to Athens itself—off the high cliffs of Cape Sounion at the very tip of Attica. There, the blasts funneling through narrow straits often churned up a caldron of clashing seas. To get under the lee of Sounion was every homesick voyager's need. Not until he rounded it could he be sure that a short day's coasting would bring him safely to little Phaleron harbor, four miles outside Athens. (Piraeus, the port that became part of the Athenian urban area, was not dredged and fortified until perhaps a thousand years after Theseus came home.)

Struggling around the dangerous promontory, we passed over a strangely dark patch of water, just below the cliff on which King Aegeus or his runner watched for the ship returning from Crete. The ship had left Athens under a blue-black sail with a bull on it, the funeral emblem of tribute. Theseus, if and when returning, was to substitute a white sail. He forgot. So Aegeus stepped to the cliff and sprang out to death. Legend says that this is why the water is forever black.

Generations of Greeks firmly believed the whole epic of Theseus. For centuries they cherished a certain old ship as the very one he had sailed. They kept it in repair. They sent it annually with sacrifices to Delos, their most sacred island. While it was away, Athens remained in a state of solemnity. (For example, the execution of Socrates was postponed until the ship came back.)

As king, Theseus unified the twelve villages on the Attica peninsula, drove off sea raiders, and cleared the roads of robbers. There is a tale of his visit to a castle atop Mount Cithaeron, which overlooked the pass to Thebes. He told the lord of the castle, "I have heard that the bed in your guest room is such a masterpiece that no man will leave it unless he is carried away. You shall lie on it yourself."

"After you," his host replied with a chuckle.

Suddenly the doors were full of Theseus's soldiers. They threw the lord's sons off the tops of the castle walls, then went to see his famous iron bed. Guests who had lain on it—those who could still crawl—begged for a chance to return their host's hospitality. When they finished with him, they dropped his corpse down the gorge. So died the last and worst of the mountain bandits, Procrustes.

Theseus went to sea again in middle age, for obscure reasons. Apparently he thought everyone loved or feared him. This was a fatal error. I followed his route across open water in the northern sea while wind blew hard from astern. I wondered if a similar wind had forced Theseus to land where he had, contrary to his plans. How often the Aegean winds, turbulent as madness, had shaped men's destinies in these islands!

In a few hours the island peaks of Skyros thrust into the sky. As we drew close I saw that they were gray and bare, like war towers. I landed, uneasy on this lonely, sharp-edged mass of rock. Long stairs were cut into it, up to where, supposedly, the home of King Lycomedes had been built under the crag like a swallow's nest. It was a perfect lookout point. I could see all over the island and, beyond, great sweeps of sea.

Lycomedes made Theseus welcome, and swapped sea tales, not bothering to hide that he often put to sea for adventure when his island harvest was poor. The two kings went for a walk, threading through the crag —and Theseus fell or was pushed. I looked down that dizzy drop, and shivered.

Athens built a temple to Theseus. As late as 476 B.C., in the skeptical age of Pericles, the city retrieved from Skyros what purported to be his remains and interred them in the temple as sacred relics. They were the bones of a warrior of imposing stature, his weapons at his side. Two years later, Athenians came back in force, demolished the stronghold, and banished the islanders, who had made piracy their trade.

So here the circling trail of Theseus ended. But here too, as in a labyrinth, I crossed the paths of other Homeric heroes. It was to Skyros that sulky young Achilles fled, hiding in the court of old King Lycomedes to avoid fighting against Troy, since there was a prophecy that he would be killed there. And it was to Skyros that wily Odysseus went, dressed as a merchant, to seek the lad. Displaying his wares to the princesses, he noticed that one girl, as it seemed, was more interested in his swords than in his fabrics and trinkets. He guessed that "she" was Achilles, and induced him to go along to Troy, where he met death as prophesied.

I cruised after them.

We rounded the knife-edged peninsula where Mount Athos stood sentinel; sighted Thasos—"bare and ugly as a donkey's back," Archilochus called it—where the plentiful gold of Troy was mined; and watched Lemnos carve the sky to starboard. This was the island where Jason and his Argonauts had dallied with women who, perhaps to prove themselves "liberated," had killed all the men on Lemnos. Knowledge of this did not repel Jason's crew: they had been at sea for a long time.

Ahead was the giant arrowhead of stone called Samothrace, its great dark cliffs and wooded bluffs looming straight up from the sea. It had no harbor, which kept it wild. But many a Greek had rowed ashore in a boat of ox hide, seeking dwarf gods who might give charms for protection from shipwreck (in return for sacrifices, of course).

We stayed well clear. We sped past the round hills of Imroz, and I felt the ship rolling in the current from the Dardanelles—or Hellespont, as men called it when Greek ships owned the seas and Trojan chariots ruled the plains.

I watched broad brown fields of Turkey slide past. That flat expanse had been "the ringing plains of windy Troy." Soon I saw the straits of Helle like the mouth of a great river. Shortly, had I been Agamemnon or Ulysses or Achilles, I would have been gazing across the water at a fearsome sight: Troy, sunning itself on its rock like an old proud lion.

I imagined the scene as the Greek armada drew near. A signal fire on the cliff would belch smoke. Bronze war gongs in the towers would be yammering. From Troy's four gates, columns of spearmen would be deploying. Dust clouds would rise as chariots rumbled onto the plain and turned toward the beach. From coves, Trojan guard galleys would sprint out, speeded by the surge of the Hellespont, to ram Agamemnon's first warships.

There would be hours of carnage on the water, on the beach, across four miles of plain. Eventually the Trojans would move back behind their great palisades.

Greek ships would loll on the sand like sea monsters gathered to spawn. The plain would swarm with Greeks digging trenches and piling stones for breastworks.

Then, for ten years, nothing much would happen. Neither army sought battle. Troy was ringed by watchfires of the invading host—but the formidable two-man two-horse Trojan chariots, fortresses on wheels, periodically made lightning-fast onslaughts, cutting paths to the citadel for supply trains or reinforcements from its allies in eastern lands. The Greeks contented themselves by sending ships to attack distant towns.

Who were the Trojans? A proud people, now lost in time.

An Egyptian papyrus mentioned them briefly as allies of the Hittites, who controlled most of present-day Turkey from a stronghold east of Ankara. Herodotus, the studious Greek often referred to as the father of history, knew little about Trojans, since he was born centuries after them, but he thought they might have been Cretans, perhaps settling at the strait after Knossos fell. Homer depicted them as speaking Greek and worshiping Greek gods.

Digging revealed that Troy was a site of not one but nine cities. Each overlay its predecessor, as if Troy had had nine lives. Communities had lived and died there; buildings fell into ruin and filled with debris; time after time a city of the living arose on a city of the dead. Perhaps no builders knew that anyone had been there before them, since centuries may have passed between the fall of one culture and the arrival of the next. Meanwhile, all traces were buried under many feet of dust and ashes.

When Schliemann excavated the site (which he located by Homer's geographical description) he found weapons and household implements, crude pots and fine vases, gewgaws, statuettes—and at last, twenty-eight feet down, a hoard of nine thousand silver and gold bracelets, brooches, buttons, chains, and diadems. In his passionate haste, Schliemann mixed up objects from various strata. He tore out walls to get at more-interesting ruins below. But others who carried on after his death, sorting through everything, eventually learned that the topmost city had been a Roman town, and that the remains at the bottom, on virgin soil, were of a village so ancient that its people used only stone tools. Sandwiched between were various undistinguished settlements and at least two different cities with thick enclosing walls that had lasted for centuries. Poseidon the Earth-Shaker had knocked down the walls of one city. Fire had blackened another.

All in all, excavations indicated that the Troy against which the Greeks sailed might have been partly Minoan, partly Mycenaean, and partly Asiatic. It was large—the wall was three miles around—and prosperous.

From the lower Aegean city-states it bought copper, olive oil, wine, and pottery. From Thrace and the Danube came amber, bronze swords, and horses. From Spain came silver, from Egypt ivory, and from distant China so great a rarity as jade. In return, Troy hauled from the interior and exported timber, silver, gold, woolen fabrics, and wild asses. Its seaport must have been as thriving as the approximately contemporary Tartessus.

In the city the houses were small and closely packed together. Storage jars were sunk deeply into floors, as if to provide for a long siege. Near the base of the walls were masses of horse bones, confirming the *Iliad*'s final line, "Thus they performed the final rites for Hector, tamer of horses." There could no longer be any doubt that the siege of Troy narrated by Homer and Virgil actually took place.

But the reasons why it took place remained unclear. H. G. Wells, in his lively *Outline of History*, accepted Homer's story at face value:

> The *Iliad* makes clear that destruction came upon Troy because Trojans stole Greek women. Modern writers, with modern ideas, have tried to make out that the Greeks assailed Troy in order to secure a trade route or some such fine-spun commercial advantage. It would be as reasonable to say that the Homeric Greeks went to war in order to be

> well ahead with a station on the Berlin-to-Baghdad railway.
>
> The Homeric Greeks were a healthy barbaric Aryan people, with very poor ideas about "trade routes"; they went to war with the Trojans because they were thoroughly annoyed about this stealing of women.

But there were doubters before modern times. Euripides, the classic dramatist, laid the war to overpopulation in the Greek lands and the consequent need for more room. So old are some modern excuses for invasions. Herodotus wasn't sure that the princess Helen really went to Troy; perhaps she went to Egypt, under her lover's constraint, and waited there for her husband, Menelaus, to rescue her. Besides, asked Herodotus, who would believe that the Trojans would endure a ten-year siege for one woman?

Yet I could believe that a story of Helen's kidnapping and rape was used to make the war appealing to common Greeks. A hundred thousand of them from all the little nations of Greece left home in a bigger fleet than any empire ever mustered before. Strong emotion must have moved them.

Their kings and sea captains probably had more practical motives. A principal business of Mycenae and her satellites seemed to be war—or, to put it plainly, piracy and conquest. According to Hittite records, marauding bands of Greeks harassed the coast of Asia Minor, on the eastern side of the Aegean, for centuries. As the hold of the Hittite empire weakened, I could visualize Mycenaean rulers growing ever more covetous.

They had trade connections with Troy and knew of its wealth. They knew also that an earthquake a few generations earlier had badly damaged its walls and towers, crippled its military forces, and bled its resources. Perhaps it took a long time to recover. So when Helen ran away with a son of the Trojan king, this gave Agamemnon a torch with which to ignite the pride of the Greeks. He took up his brother's quarrel with the

Trojans and used all his influence to muster forces from the Greek kingdoms.

Of course, the prospective sack of Troy could never provide loot enough for such a huge expeditionary force. Even though "trade routes" meant nothing to them, Agamemnon's allies could have reached and robbed fat Thrace and other inland cities, once the Trojans were gone. Troy commanded the mouth of the Hellespont and the rich lands around the Black Sea. The gray lion on its rock was perfectly placed to extort tolls from ships wishing to pass through the Hellespont, or to close the strait to them altogether.

That strait had long fascinated the sailors of the Aegean Sea. They yearned to see the unknown country beyond, at the back of the north wind, where the legendary Golden Fleece lay. This was the subject of one of the oldest sagas handed down, the voyage of the Argonauts—notable because Greeks talked of it as their first major seafaring venture, and because it enrolled so many illustrious figures. No list survived of those who accompanied Jason into the Black Sea on the good ship *Argo;* innumerable Greek families claimed, as they climbed to prominence in later centuries, that an ancestor had been aboard, as if it were a kind of *Mayflower*. Pindar and later poets, culling the legends, agreed that the expedition had included such glamorous figures as the inseparable twins Castor and Pollux, the demigod musician Orpheus, and the mighty Hercules.

Apparently, Jason, a dashing pirate captain, set sail in his swift fifty-oared longship to force the Hellespont. As the vessel entered the strait it was halted, seemingly by Trojans, for Hercules went ashore to run amok in Troy and kill its king and all his sons but Priam. The Argonauts rowed on, seized the Fleece after many perils, and found a way home via the Danube and the Adriatic Sea.

The Fleece was supposedly the pure gold skin of a winged ram. A myth may be a bit of wisdom personified in symbolic figures, as the story of Eden suggests the disillusionment of knowledge and the liabilities of love. Or it may be a scrap of history embroidered in word-of-mouth transmission. I surmised that in the generation before the siege of Troy, the Greeks tried to force their way into the Black Sea to loot; the tale of the Argonauts could be a dramatized memory of that venture, and the Golden Fleece could have been sheepskins, which in ancient times were used in northern Turkey to catch grains of gold carried down by the streams.

Anyhow, Troy must have pulled itself together after Hercules's visitation and resumed its blockade of the Hellespont. But the Greeks didn't forget. They would come again, a thousand ships instead of one. And on the plains of Troy the Greek nations would destroy themselves to free the Hellespont.

The dark teeth of the Trojan fortress were unbreakable. The Greeks never came close to penetrating by force. After ten years they were on the verge of going home, when a goddess inspired a seer with the stratagem commemorated by Homer and Virgil and also in many earlier Greek vase paintings and bas-reliefs.

The Greeks built a huge wooden horse, concealed their bravest soldiers inside, and left it outside Troy as a peace offering. They vacated their camp, and went into hiding, whereupon the Trojans dragged the horse into their towered city. In a victorious mood, they ignored their chronic doom-sayer Cassandra, who warned that a horse would ruin them. They scoffed at their priest Laocoon, who cried, "Beware of Greeks bearing gifts!" In the dead of night the Greeks emerged and opened the gates. Troy was sacked, its men slaughtered, its treasures plundered, its women and children dragged off as slaves.

I could visualize the night. There was plenty to burn: oil and grain were stored; the stone-walled houses had thatched roofs and doors and furniture and thick wooden beams. Soon the greatest pyre that men ever lit was burning. Priam's marble throne was turning black, and the blue dolphins were leaping on a sea of fire, and the Cretan reeds were crackling. Someone swept together hundreds of gold baubles in a box, and tried to flee, only to be crushed by a rock falling from the palace wall. The box was buried under the debris, for Schliemann to find three thousand years later.

When the glow climbed the night sky, other fires were lit far away. One leaped from a peak in the Rhodope Mountains. In a great curve to the west, lights flickered from Imroz and Samothrace and Thasos and Parnassus. Wood had been piled years ago to await this moment.

In Mycenae, atop Agamemnon's palace, a slave who had lain nightly on the roof throughout the war stared north at a blazing signal and then stumbled down to give the news to the queen and her lover.

All around the Aegean the balefires proclaimed that Troy had fallen. At Pella an illiterate chief saw the fires and fingered the edge of his sword. Tribesmen in the mountains of Thessaly and Macedonia sniffed the sudden warm wind and looked down to the rich lands whence it blew.

A world burned itself out that night around the dark sea, and soon a tide of iron would be creeping down ravines toward Tiryns and Mycenae and Argos. The highlands had grown a crop of fighters more grim than Homer's heroes.

They battered open the lordly palaces. At Mycenae, archaeologists found evidence that defenses had been hurriedly strengthened and the water supply protected. But the city perished. It left no records. Only the mute stones stood witness to whatever happened. At Tiryns the evidence was dramatic—at the foot of the city walls, buried beneath ashes and charcoal, the skeletons of the last defenders lay where they had fallen or been thrown.

Half-civilized tribes from the north, called Dorians, were overrunning central Greece and Peloponnesus. They came with iron weapons, herds of cattle, and wagon trains carrying their women and children. They meant to stay, and they did. They put nobles to the sword and turned townspeople into serfs.

Some Greeks got away into the mountains of Arcadia, some into Attica, some to islands, some to the coasts of Asia. The invaders followed them into Attica, but were repelled at the small city of Athens; they followed to Crete, and made final the destruction of Knossos; they captured and colonized Thera and other isles.

By about 1100 B.C., high civilization was confined mainly to its earlier homes in Egypt and Mesopotamia. Asia Minor was in darkness. Greece forgot the art of writing. The history of Crete and Mycenae vanished into dim legend. Time had run out for the Bronze Age.

The Dorians practiced no arts and few crafts and trades. They squatted in burnt-out palaces but built nothing there, preferring farm and village life. Each valley had its huddle of huts, and every huddle owed fealty to a local chieftain. Sometimes one village fought another for good bottom land, but not for glory. Every man, feeling unsafe, carried arms. Life was chaos as families wandered, seeking security and peace.

This terminal catastrophe in the prehistory of civilization around the Aegean is what modern historians call "the Dorian conquest" and "the first Dark Age of Europe." The darkness lasted about four hundred years.

Through those centuries there were trickles of migration—mostly to the stronghold of Athens, which never fell to the Dorian hordes because of its natural fortress, the rocky Acropolis. Eventually the population grew too large for the limited space. So Greeks began sailing in small craft to start new settlements in the Cyclades Islands, and later along the west coast of Asia Minor. This new extension of Greece came to be called Ionia.

The refugees brought with them an ancient tradition of song. Somewhere in Ionia a blind Greek named Homer began to wander, singing lays of great deeds done long ago, set to the music of his lyre.

Of this man we know next to nothing. He said not a word about himself in the versions of his songs that were eventually written down by others and preserved for us. But somehow he looked back with clear vision on vistas of time. He led the Greeks out of twilight and into a brilliant scene of bygone glory. And it was all vivid and concrete. He didn't spin yarns of highly improbable persons in a vague landscape somewhere outside time and known space. He narrated particular episodes of one particular war in which many heroes fought—all listed in Book II of the *Iliad* together with their cities of origin, the strength of their cohorts, and the number of their ships.

Homer told about these heroes in remarkable detail: their weapons, manual skills, their dress; he even gave menus of their banquets and summaries of their speeches at councils of war. It was as if he had been with them. But remember, he was born centuries later. In his time, none of their artifacts and written records were extant.

In the *Iliad* and sometimes even in the *Odyssey,* narrating the far wanderings of Odysseus after the war, Homer's descriptions of places had a wealth of topographical detail. He named mountains, districts, harbors, and springs. He pictured specific landscapes so vividly that I wondered how tradition could suggest that he was blind. (Yet he thought sea water was the same color as wine, a mistake only a blind man would be likely to make.)

His story in the *Iliad* was almost without geographic error. Though many of the facts seem unimportant to modern readers—like the course of the Scamander as it ran then, or the distance from the city to the Greek camp, or the plants and bushes on the plain—they prove that he knew more about the battlefield than anyone in his day could have learned by visiting the long-buried site.

Homer even knew facts about towers and gates of Troy, and, more surprisingly, about the structure of its walls. He knew the techniques of siege craft, which had been forgotten before his time. He knew that among the Trojan cohorts were people who looked like Hittites.

Homer was the subject of the world's longest scholarly debate in the era when the Trojan War was assumed to be merely a poetic fancy. Some experts said there was no such person as Homer; the *Iliad* and the *Odyssey* were collections of fiction written by a number of authors. Of course, Homer left nothing in writing to prove his authorship. But the debate subsided as evidence of his existence came to light, and archaeological digs confirmed details of his epics. His ways of obtaining those details still are baffling. He must have had access to some vast store of knowledge from a remote past—almost as if he were psychic, like our own time's Edgar Cayce.

To his unlettered countrymen, struggling to regain a lost glory, puzzling over cryptic carvings and ruins without names, Homer's epics were inspiration, education, and entertainment. They were recited incessantly (and carefully, word for word) by minstrels in a society that remained illiterate for centuries. They became the source book of Greek religion. They were a foundation of Greek history, philosophy, drama, poetry, and science.

Homer dared to use Greek gods as comic relief. They controlled much of the action in the *Iliad* and the *Odyssey,* arbitrarily and for reasons ranging from all-too-human to contemptible. Homer's gods were eccentrics who happened to possess powers similar to those of today's Superman and Wonder Woman. Did the poet himself believe in those gods? That is another of his secrets. Undoubtedly his listeners believed.

Contemporaries of Plato and Aristotle accepted his story of Troy as real. It remained real to the generations that followed. When Alexander the Great crossed the Hellespont on his way to war with the Persians, he stopped to view the site of Troy, and was shown a shield supposedly carried by Achilles nearly a thousand years before. He piously removed it and took it with him into battle from Palestine to Punjab. Caesar too paid homage before the ruins and burned incense to the gods. Centuries later, Constantine thought of building his empire's new eastern capital at Troy, but settled on Byzantium instead.

The first texts of Homer's epics could have been written down soon after 750 B.C., or much later. Not until about 270 B.C. did Zenodotus, the pioneer librarian, compile the first scholarly edition of Homer. It put the text substantially in the form from which all English translations were rendered.

Behind Homer moved older, darker forms, stretching back unknown distances. Some students saw Homeric myths as legacies from other civilizations. The famous Twelve Labors of Hercules seem to be connected with the twelve signs of the zodiac, which originated with Babylon no later than 2000 B.C. Perhaps certain Greeks knew more about astronomy than the textbooks reveal. Anaxagoras, about 450 B.C., was the first man we know of to suggest that the moon was made of rocky material similar to that of the earth. For this and other impious notions, he was banished from Athens.

In 1901 divers working off a Greek isle found the wreck of an ancient ship. Among the items aboard was the most complex scientific object ever recovered from antiquity. Corroded and crumbling from centuries in salt water, the object was a clocklike mechanism with dials and inscribed plates. A remarkably complex assembly of twenty gear wheels was mounted inside. From the markings, the mechanism was identified as a device for calculating motions of stars and planets. Nothing like it has ever been found elsewhere. Nothing comparable is known from any ancient scientific text or literary allusion. On the contrary, from all that survived of the science and technology of classical Greece, experts would have said that such a device *couldn't* exist. All other known contraptions from that civilization were crude and unsophisticated. This was a tantalizing clue to an unseen side of Greek life—one more mystery about the lost peoples who once lived around the Aegean Sea.

# 8

# When Death Was Fun

I walked through a city of the dead: street after street of echoing underground houses, every room containing remains of long-dead people.

I found it a delightful experience.

These dead were interred under statues of themselves, and the statues looked happy and lifelike. The rooms were cheerful, with walls brightened by paintings of early life: hunting, feasting, dancing, boating.

The city, called Cerveteri, wasn't the only one of its kind. I also explored Tarquinia, Vulci, and other abandoned sites of the same civilization. Each was a huge cemetery—almost all that remained of this civilization, but worth visiting. Altogether, I thought, these were the pleasantest and most interesting burial places in the world. Forest Lawn and Westminster Abbey were dull by comparison.

Even above ground the site was strangely charming, although there was nothing to be seen but great grassy mounds with ancient stone borders. Larks chirped and fluttered. Strolling along the central walk, I felt soothed, as if just being there was good for my soul.

It was the same when I went down the few dark steps into the subterranean burial city. Its streets and crossways were swept bare; the inhabitants were "asleep," leaving everything ready for the next comer. They had created an atmosphere of happiness and hominess.

Cut from living rock, the houses were much like those of living people. Each ceiling had a beam carved to imitate the roof beam of above-ground houses. Hanging on walls were skillets and pans, bellows for the fire, weapons for hunting—all bas-reliefs, yet reasonable facsimiles. Treasures of jewelry and goldwork had also been in some tombs, as at Mycenae, but these had been looted or put in museums centuries ago.

Some of the statues were damaged, yet the feeling of real life lingered. Fragments of people at banquets, limbs that danced without dancers, birds in flight on one wing, dogs whose heads were worn away—all seemed charged with a sense of playfulness.

Down there in the silence of eternity, as I walked from home to home I saw enough intact or nearly intact statues to get vivid ideas of who slept beneath. A husband and wife sat on a coffin lid, holding hands, seeming to enjoy each other's presence. A magistrate strode along, robe rippling; bailiffs preceded him with rods, and clerks followed with scrolls. Schoolgirls attended class, mothers fondled babies, young sweethearts proffered loving cups, a warrior clutched chariot reins.

And then the paintings. They infused rooms with airy lightness, as if another sun shone in the underworld. The faded colors were still fresh: sky-blue, grass-green, orange, ocher-red—the colors of spring. The tomb walls were covered with a thin coat of stucco, weathered to a creamy gold, a beautiful color for background.

The scenes depicted were lively and festive. Dancers whirled, a boy dove into the wavy edge of the sea, a girl at a banquet threw her arms around the neck of her lover, a flute player blew his double pipes like Pan, smiling slaves sprang to lift wine jars.

Looking closely at these paintings brought the people more alive in my mind. They were tanned and ruddy, short, with thick massive limbs. Despite their heavyset physiques they moved with a strange, powerful alertness in those dim frescoes. They danced nimbly; cavorting arms and legs showed pleasure in life. The movements surged from within like strong tides. These people were charged with energy, drawing from deep currents foreign to the shallows of most lives—as if electrified by sources we could never reach.

They got into my imagination and would not go out. I had to know more about them. Since their tombs were so gay, what must their lives have been?

These were the Etruscans, a shadow people met today only in their tombs or in museum halls. Although closer in time, they are less accessible than the people of ancient Egypt, Mesopotamia, Crete, or Mycenae. Even after decades of intense study, linguists cannot read their language—and few of their writings survived anyhow, though they were known to have written enormously.

Moreover, Etruria produced no Homer. In other words, the Etruscans, unlike the Greeks and some Africans and several other peoples, lacked glorious legends passed along by bards through many centuries. Seven hundred years of Etruscan history existed only in biased summaries by their enemies, the Greeks and the Romans, who outlasted them.

The Etruscans arrived during the time of the great folk wanderings that marked the end of the Bronze Age. Dorians had demolished preclassical Greece and blotted out the ancient cultures of Crete and Mycenae. In what is now Italy, nameless tribes and clans moved like shadows over the land, leaving almost no trace. One last wave of these Indo-European tribesmen, the Latins, entered Italy eight or nine centuries before Christ. They built huts and tilled land in the Alban hills. These were to become the Romans.

Sometime in the eighth century B.C. the Etruscans

probably came to Italy by sea. On the west coast, above the Tiber River, they put up solid rock forts of the old Mycenaean type. Finding iron deposits, they started a metal industry, and forged spears and swords better than those of any other people of that time. Their superior killing power enabled them to spread inland, gradually subduing the tribes they met between the Tiber and the Alps. They sent fleets to sea, sailing boldly along the coasts of Provence, Spain, and North Africa, mixing trading with piracy.

In so doing they often collided with Greeks and Carthaginians, whom they fought with zest and success. Iron gave their ships piercing prows; iron armed their crews with battle-axes and grappling hooks and shields.

These formidable and gifted newcomers called themselves Rasenna, although the Latin name for them was Etruscans, which meant "pirates." They were by far the most civilized people on the Italian peninsula.

The homeland they acquired wasn't then the smiling land of vineyards and olive trees it would become. It was forest and malarial swamps. Etruscan engineers tunneled through hills to let out the overflow of lakes. They put down roads as fine as anything achieved by the Romans centuries later—well drained and engineered to take heavy traffic across woods and rocks. Their chariots were big and splendid with heavily embossed decorations, like one I saw in the Metropolitan Museum of Art in New York.

Soon Etruscan towns arose on reclaimed land—not clumps of huts as before them, but walled communities in geometric patterns with two main intersecting thoroughfares, a plan that the Romans would imitate in military camps as well as in cities. In building, the Etruscans used stone only for defense, and created comfortable houses of sun-dried brick or timber. They gave careful thought to heating and hydraulics. Their systems of urban sewage disposal and rural irrigation were beyond anything discovered in contemporary Carthage or Greece.

I could visualize the stocky, sun-browned Etruscan warriors marching smartly along their military roads in the triple formation of light, medium, and heavy infantry, which was later copied by the Roman legions. During the seventh and sixth centuries B.C. they were carving out a small empire of their own, reaching northward up the Po Valley, southward against the resurgent Greeks' towns in Sicily and lower Italy.

By about 600 B.C. the Etruscan civilization was in full bloom. A number of Etruscan cities were minting their own coins. There never was a unified empire, only a loose federation of about fifty wealthy city-states, each led by its own feudal lord. He was both priest and general. In times of war—which were rare—he put on a demon mask and led the way, carrying a torch and live snakes to hurl at foes.

Wars were few in that century. Greece and Carthage prudently chose to parley and trade with Etruscans rather than fight them. The Etruscan federation never waged an organized war. Once their cities were entrenched, neither expansion nor hegemony seemed to suit their temperament.

For some reason, that temperament grew visibly gloomier with the centuries, impelling Etruscans not into empire building but into slow decline. I saw this in the tombs.

I went through in rough chronological order, starting at the oldest and working toward the most recent. It was eerie to see the paintings become less joyous as I went along. A few people still were shown dancing, but they no longer seemed to celebrate an eternity at home; they went dancing and fluting along through little olive trees and out into some other, unknowable continuum.

Banquet scenes were quieter but still pleasant, until I sensed sadness. I studied a bearded man gently touching a woman under the chin. The delicate caress was charming. These people enjoyed the sense of touch for the sake of being really in contact, I thought. In the faded fresco was a quiet flow from finger to chin that united the man and woman.

Later, revellers were languid or libidinous. There was lazy pawing and laying hold. Women's looks were free and bold.

Sculptures showed the people becoming fatter. They lolled on cushions and looked into wine cups. One couple went boating on a slow stream. I couldn't fathom their faces: solemn but not entirely sad, they seemed resigned, enigmatic.

Another few generations, and the painted scenes turned morbid. Among hovering birds I saw mourners before blood-red gates; these symbolized the barrier between our world and the kingdom of death, I was told. Animals crowded into the pictures. First leopards with tongues hanging out, and cringing deer. Then malevolent creatures—sphinxes, chimeras, griffins—lurking in gables of tombs, crouching in the friezes around the walls. I saw a few grinning popeyed demons with snaky hair, presumably gorgons. Apparently, these later Etruscans knew Greek myths.

Another Greek creation began to appear in murals: Charon. But he wasn't the benign old ferryman of classic legend. He was a monster with a wolf's head and bluish skin like decaying flesh. He bore a big hammer, ready to crush the skulls of the doomed before he dragged them onto his boat.

Massacres and bloody duels dominated the final century of funerary paintings. One showed captives being stoned to death. In another, a gladiator, unarmed but with a fierce dog beside him, fought a blindfolded opponent who swung a club. Human sacrifice scenes became common. Maidens were ritually slaughtered while deities watched.

Then there were no more tombs. I had reached the end of a civilization. I had seen all there was of its history, except what could be deduced from references in other languages, and a few archaeological finds outside the cemeteries.

I delved into these. First I wanted to know where the Etruscans had come from.

The Greek traveler and historian Herodotus was sure he knew. Writing in the fifth century B.C., when the Etruscans were supreme in Italy, he said they had lived in Lydia (today, southwest Turkey) and left it because of a long famine. But another Greek historian, Dionysius of Halicarnassus, who himself came from that Turkish region, contradicted Herodotus four centuries later. He insisted that the Etruscans were simply a sudden flowering of intermingled native tribes who had always lived in Italy.

In his time, the Etruscan language was still spoken by a few refugees, and their sacred books and traditional histories still existed. He pointed out that the people neither spoke the Lydian language nor worshiped Lydian gods. (Oddly, they often displayed the double-ax emblem as a symbol of kingly power in court proceedings, reproduced in tomb murals and sculptures. Probably the Greek historians never knew that this was also the emblem of the bygone Minoan kings.)

Lydia was the most powerful of numerous nations between the Hellespont and Syria. Sardis, the capital, was famous, as its ruins still suggest. Its kings still merit a line or two in textbooks of ancient history—particularly Croesus, the last ruler of the kingdom (565–546 B.C.), who ruled all of western Asia Minor, collecting tribute from a host of subject peoples and thus amassing the wealth for which he was remembered. When the Persians came, they apparently burned him alive as a sacrifice to their victorious gods.

I could believe that Etruscans were Asiatics from Lydia or from one of its vassal states. Their paintings and statuary showed them with slanting, almond-shaped eyes. Their own name for themselves, Rasenna, turned up in various forms in prehistoric Turkey. And on the island of Lemnos, in the Aegean, I had seen inscriptions in an unknown language that, linguists said, was remarkably like ancient Etruscan. (Did Lydia have two languages?) If starving Etruscans fled from behind the Hellespont, some of them could easily have stayed on Lemnos, a few miles off the coast. Too, Lydia was on the great road that joined Mesopotamia with the eastern Mediterranean; this could account for signs of Assyrian influence, like the spade beards shown in some Etruscan tombs, and for certain other folkways that seemed Babylonian. For example, Babylonians and other Oriental peoples were totally submissive to their gods. So were Etruscans.

Submissive to the gods! Was this a key to the strange decline of Etruria after such a successful and happy debut?

Wherever these mysterious people came from, they were civilized when they first appeared on Italy's coast—or else they suddenly acquired civilization. (People who are advanced enough to cross a sea to start a new life usually do extraordinarily well.) Anyhow, the Etruscans ruled Rome for its first hundred years, and left so many imprints on Roman ways that Rome could barely be understood without them. Yet Roman literature was as silent about them as a matron trying to ignore her indiscreet girlhood.

Etruscans made Rome a city. Despite a hallowed legend that *Roma* derived from *Romulus,* the word seemed to be Etruscan. Later-day Italians maintained that Romulus and his brother founded Rome in 753 B.C., but Etruscan tombs found beneath the Roman Forum were proved to be much older than that. And the so-called tomb of Romulus bore an Etruscan inscription.

Perhaps the Latins, still farmers, sent a posse to seize the site of Rome as a strategic moat against the expanding Etruscans. It was where an easy fording of the Tiber could be guarded by adjacent heights. A sort of trading post got started, where Latins and Etruscans bartered, but nobody lived there permanently. Wanderers found asylum and employment at this mart, so some of them settled on the seven hills overlooking it. (The ford itself was a lake in the rainy season.) One by one the slopes were peopled. In time the settlements merged into a town that would become the most famous of man's habitations.

It was twenty miles from the sea and not suited for maritime commerce—but in those days of marauding ships, towns were safer when situated a bit inland. For internal trade Rome was well placed at the crossroads of traffic on the river and the north–south land route. Etruscan engineers built Rome's walls and sewers, turning it from a swamp into a protected and sanitary city, and probably built Rome's first edifices of wood, brick, and stone. Not till Caesar would Rome see as much building as under its first kings, the Tarquins, who were Etruscan.

But Etruscans never considered Rome their capital. They had no capital. Their oldest and mightiest city was Cortona, supposedly built before Troy. Its bulky two-mile walls, circling the town, can still be seen. Tarquinia was their most studious city; Roman aristocrats sent sons there, from the seventh to the fourth century B.C., to absorb Etruscan knowledge as diligently as they later did the Greek; among other things they learned geometry, surveying, and architecture. Roman builders got the arch from the Etruscans—who either invented it or inherited it from Mesopotamia through some intermediary.

Those were sunny centuries for the Etruscans. Their tomb art implied that they lived luxuriously and enjoyed life; they sang and played musical instruments night and day, even as accompaniment to baking bread or whipping slaves. They gave women honored places at home and in society. They were extremely knowledgeable; the great Roman encyclopedist, Marcus Terentius Varro, announced that he used Etruscan texts in compiling his 490 books, which covered every field of science and art—and which were tragically lost to posterity sometime after 1320 A.D., probably because churchmen burned them.

Of all European peoples the Etruscans were the ones most given to religious rites—convinced, perhaps, that their ceremonies got good results in this world and in the next. They were a merry people as far as death was concerned, never jibbing at blood and carnage. They believed themselves blessed by their old nature gods, who promised them eternal life in a pleasant afterworld. Thus, for them, death was the beginning of a journey, and only a temporary parting from loved ones. Departure scenes were typical on funeral urns in Volterra, one of the first Etruscan cities. The dead were depicted as starting a trip on horseback or in covered wagons drawn by horses. Husbands or wives and children and friends were taking leave of the traveler. Sometimes the separation was symbolized by a half-open door through which the departing touched hands with those staying behind.

No other people cherished and guarded their dead as the Etruscans did. No other people provided such cheery surroundings for them. Mausoleums were equipped with everything they might need or desire. (Priests taught that if a spirit was discontented, it would leave its tomb to haunt the living.) So these tombs were designed for magical purposes; obviously, a shade couldn't cook with a stone saucepan carved on the wall, but by magic he would convert it for his uses.

There was intended magic, too, in the funeral rites. Customarily the unburied corpse was guest of honor at a lavish banquet in its new home. Funeral games took place to entertain it. Blood of animals and humans was poured to reinvigorate it. Knowing that all this would be done for him, any Etruscan presumably welcomed death.

How did such a happy faith turn gloomy? Part of the answer, I thought, lay in the influence of the rising Greek civilization.

Etruscans adopted the Greek concept of an underworld beyond the River Styx, but apparently felt no need to reconcile the two theologies, for their funerary rites didn't seem to change much. But they also learned from the Greeks that gods could be fickle and cruel, and this worried them deeply.

Unlike the Greeks, the Etruscans became obsessed with religion. They never made the leap from superstition to scientific investigation. Submissively, with minds closed, they obeyed their sacred books (which contained no moral tenets, apparently) and their priests.

Etruscan priests studied omens ever more anxiously, seeking ways to please the gods and read the future. If some priests spoke for gods in ways that strengthened themselves or weakened their potential enemies, who was to know? As long as they could find subterranean water with divining rods, as Romans wrote they often did, they were acknowledged as infallible.

Romans as well as Etruscans felt sure that Etruscan priests, called *haruspices* (from which we get our word *auspices*), were very learned in the arts of augury, or ascertaining the future. These arts, including especially studying entrails of animals, derived from the old, old East. They were expounded by Babylonians and later adopted by Hittites. Baked-clay models of livers, found by excavators in the Holy Land, indicated that the art was taught there too. This confirmed an Old Testament reference where Ezekiel (21:21) said, "The King of Babylon stood at the parting of the way, at the head of the two ways, to use divination. . . . He looked in the liver."

In the livers of sheep, in the flight of birds, in the behavior of thunder and lightning, a *haruspex* saw a purported picture of the past and future as a unified whole—much as modern weather forecasters and economists seek to do from studying other signals.

When a *haruspex* saw that disaster impended, he suggested ways in which it might be postponed or softened, although he admitted that his suggestions weren't sure to work. The workings of the gods (which had little to do with sin and punishment, in Etruscan theology) were like the tides and the seasons. Nothing happened by chance. The far future was ordained, so men must adjust as best they could. Divination would help them foresee and adjust.

Did these *haruspices* really have supernatural insight sometimes? How else, I wondered, could they have gripped men's minds for century after century? Romans never forgot that when the third and last Etruscan king of their city was dethroned in 510 B.C., Etruscan soothsayers predicted that Rome would one day be "the head of all," and it came to pass. Nor did they forget that Julius Caesar kept an Etruscan *haruspex*, Spurinna, who warned him in vain against the Ides of March in 44 B.C.

These diviners, who wore conical brimmed hats like our Halloween witches' hats, enjoyed special protection for centuries after all other Etruscans disappeared. In 47 A.D. the Roman senate established an order of *haruspices* as a college to hand down their heavenly lore to their sons. They were still an official part of every Roman army right up until the end of Roman paganism; they held honored places beside Emperor Julian in 363 A.D. Even in 408 A.D., when Rome was threatened by Visigoth hordes, Pope Innocent let a *haruspex* try to conjure up lightning, either to frighten the enemy or to foreshadow the future. (No lightning came, and the barbarians sacked Rome.)

As for the ordinary lay Etruscans, their religion led them slowly down to limbo. It taught that in the life of nations and of men there is birth, maturity, and death. This was set forth in a religious document, mentioned in Roman writings as the *Libri Fatales* (Books of Destiny), which gave man a life-span of seven periods, flexible in length but adding up to a maximum of eighty-four years. Anyone who outlived that age was assumed to be inwardly dead anyhow.

Somehow this made the prospect of death—even if preceded by pain—more intoxicating. Early in their history the Etruscans enjoyed risking themselves. They hunted, fought bulls, and drove their chariots, sometimes four horses abreast, around dangerous courses. They boxed with spikes on their knuckles. They apparently thought they were safe until there came a predestined time for their end. Or were they seduced by subconscious death wishes? Was there a streak of masochism in them?

In their decadence, the Etruscans' love of death was perverted into lust for the death of others. They delighted in slaughtering criminals and war captives instead of enslaving them. They enlivened funerals with human sacrifices. The more brutality and blood, the more invigorated their honored dead would be—or so they thought, to judge from the paintings.

At last they hit on a way of deriving even more fun from death: combat between gladiators. They made it part of funeral rites to force prisoners into mortal combat before gleeful spectators. Tomb paintings commemorated men fighting bears, dogs, and each other.

This was virtually unique in the whole of humanity's history. Many civilizations staged public maimings and executions. Others put on fights between animals ranging from crickets to elephants. Medieval Europe and India prescribed public duels to settle quarrels and lawsuits. The Spaniards paid matadors well. Only the Etruscans, so far as we know, thought of "games" in which men fought and died to glorify the gods and entertain religious congregations.

In 264 B.C. the Romans picked up the idea, but without the religious excuse. The Circus Maximus and the Colosseum were operated simply to gratify mobs and advance the promoters. But the Etruscan origin of the idea was clear throughout Roman history: someone wearing the distinctive mask of an Etruscan demon of the underworld was always on hand to drag off gladiators killed in combat.

Meanwhile, Etruria died. It expected to.

*Haruspices* had long taught that their nation—like all nations—had a life of ten chapters, after which it would disappear. The chapters were to be about a century each, but conceivably as short as eighty years. This was comforting during the first seven hundred years. From then on it was a prophecy of imminent doom. The diviners found no way to ease Etruria out of the psychic trap.

Any omen—a plague of mice, an earthquake, a discoloring of the Tiber—might mark a chapter's end. Priests studied the signs to discover their meaning. As the presumed "tenth chapter" drew closer, Etruscan soldiers went to war with little hope of victory, and youngsters went to school with no ambition.

The long struggle between the Etruscans and the new city on the Tiber wasn't described in detail in any history that came down to us. The Etruscans were better armed, more dashing, and more numerous. It might have been hard for the Romans if they had fought alone. But two disasters befell the Etruscans, so weakening them that the Romans eventually overcame them altogether.

The first of these was a war with the Greek city-state Syracuse, in Sicily, which destroyed the Etruscan fleet in 474 B.C. The second was a great raid by the Gauls from the north into Italy, toward the end of that same century. The Etruscan federation gradually fell apart under alternate hammer blows of Romans and Gauls.

The Etruscans were a long time dying out as a people. Greek colonists and Carthaginians stole away their commerce. Gauls overwhelmed their northern outposts. Rome took their high-walled cities one by one—sometimes because of apparent treachery within, since there were surrenders without even token resistance, and surprises from tunnels under walls.

Romans had learned well from their Etruscan tutors. They arrayed their infantry in three tight ranks as the Etruscans did, and used Etruscan-designed weapons and armor. Adding Etruscan techniques to their own fortitude and talent for organization, they supplanted their teachers as the mightiest fighting force in Europe.

Rome admitted that the Etruscans fought bravely, even madly, in the last great battle at the Vadimon Lake. Perhaps these Etruscans, being sure that death was predestined, chose to make a pretty death by taking many Romans with them.

By 250 B.C. Roman soldiers were garrisoned in all Etruscan towns, interbreeding with the residents. A century later, funeral inscriptions were being written in Latin throughout the land. Some deserted Etruscan towns were plundered of their stones, so almost nothing remained. On the sites of others, Roman cities arose with new names.

Many Etruscans survived until 82 B.C., when Sulla ordered a general massacre. In Christ's time the Etruscan language was dead, except among those people who had fled to the hills. By the second century A.D. no one spoke Etruscan or preserved the sacred books.

The civilization didn't survive even in memory. Rome's emperor Claudius compiled a twenty-volume history of it, but all his writings were later lost. From the end of the Roman Empire until the end of the Middle Ages, the Etruscans were as unknown as the Sumerians, Hittites, Phoenicians, and countless other peoples of prehistory.

But the Etruscan underground cities of tombs still

existed. In Victorian times, the first sensational discoveries revealed the wealth sealed up underground, and thousands of tombs were dug out. Some treasures went into museums, some into private collections, some into thieves' markets. But the Etruscans remained enigmatic, their thought and history untold.

I wondered if this would always be so. Across twenty-five centuries their sensitive, worldly faces regarded me with ironic amusement, half smiling as if they wished I knew their secrets.

Where are they now?
The dead souls,
the fabulous treasures,
the great cities…
What really happened?

# The Search for Vilcabamba-the Ancient

In 1911 Hiram Bingham thought he had discovered Vilcabamba, but what he found was Machu Picchu–a fortress perched on a mountaintop.

In 1976 Professor Edmundo Guillen located what is believed to be the real Vilcabamba under 400 years' of vegetation.

Surviving pieces of gold indicate that there
is a gigantic horde of gold and silver buried somewhere.

Grave robbers are still at work in Peru seeking the legendary gold.

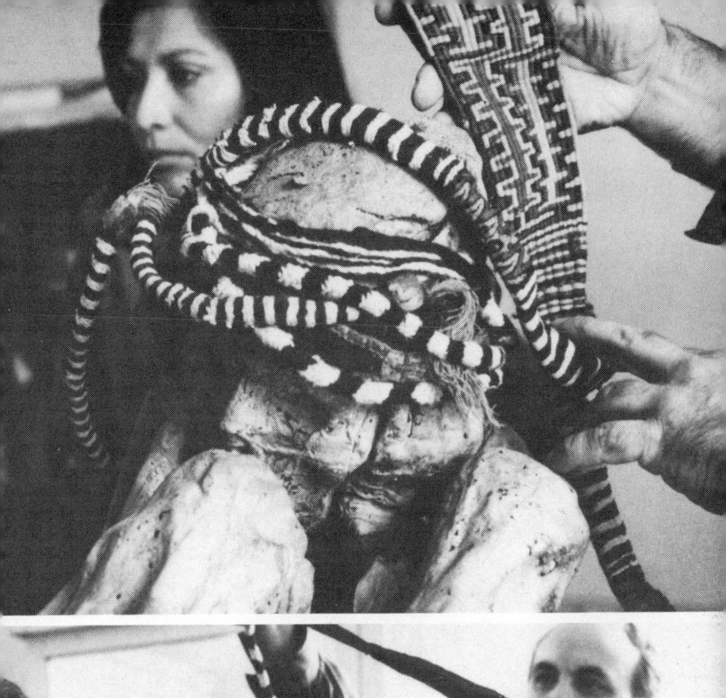

The last Incan ruler withdrew to Vilcabamba in the face of the Spanish onslaught. With him went an enormous trove of gold and silver. Legend has it that he is buried with his gold. Here is the discovery and unwrapping of a mummy who turned out to be a simple tailor with samples of his work tied around his head.

# The Search for Atlantis

BIMINI The Bimini Wall might be a deserted city. An Atlantis theory could explain these well-engineered stone structures under 35 feet of water.

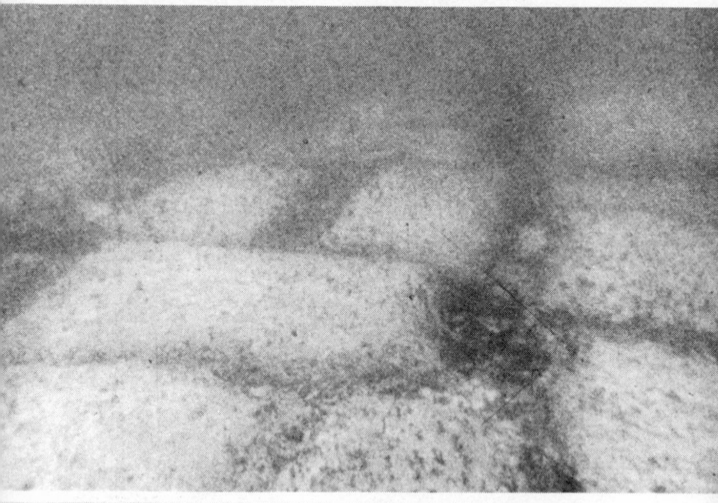

THERA In 1956 a discovery convinced some that Thera, in the Aegean Sea, could have been the center of the fabled empire of Atlantis. This civilization disappeared around 1400 B.C.

Excavations unearthed a 3-tiered city, including a villa whose interior walls bear glowing floral motifs.

ɩrchaeologists burrowed into underground structures containing scoes, pottery and artwork unlike anything from classical Greece.

**CRETE** There is a theory that legends of Atlantis were garbled descriptions of Minoan Crete. Who were the Minoans? Where did they come from? Where did they go? Their end is a mystery.

Knossos, the ruined city of ancient Crete, is 5 or more stories high. On the upper levels were spacious chambers. In the dim depths was the labyrinth in which King Minos kept the monstrous Minotaur.

The Hall of the Colonnades in the Palace of Minos has restored courtyards, stairways and colonnades.

Could the Minoans have sailed all the way to prehistoric America? At Mystery Hill, New Hampshire, there is a stone labyrinth. The inscriptions on the walls resemble Minoan hieroglyphs.

# Lost Tribes

**MYCENAE** The Gate of Lions, now worn and headless, stands guard over a long-gone grandeur.

The stone gateway to the entrance of Agamemnon's tomb. Carved from a single piece of stone, the crosspiece is a larger building unit than any used in Egyptian pyramids. Yet somehow the Mycenaeans maneuvered it onto stone uprights without cranes or jacks, and fitted it neatly into place, where it stayed for 3000 years.

The Mycenaeans were spectacular builders. These mighty ramparts are 30 feet thick in some places. The natives called the walls "cyclopean."

CERVETERI In this subterranean burial city, the dead were interred under statues of
themselves. Etruscan gladiatorial death combats were inspiration for the later Roman games.

Much of the tomb art commemorated fighting men
and a luxurious lifestyle.

**STONEHENGE** Stonehenge, in southern England, was an astronomical observatory and 56-year calendar. Did the Stone Age Britains gather this evidence for the priest-rulers in Egypt, Sumer, Crete or Mycenae? Did these civilizations send expeditions to England to construct the stones?

Today, members of a "Most Ancient Order of Druids" meet at Stonehenge and perform secret ceremonies that they say date back to Atlantis.

**EASTER ISLAND**
Who erected these stone
statues, some as
tall as 3-story houses?
The largest of
the monoliths gazes
sternly inland.

Other sculptures march toward
the sea and their final resting place.

DOGONS The Dogons believed they had descended from a star called Sirius. How could a so-called primitive tribe discover a star invisible to the naked eye?
The Dogon villages look like huge pieces of pottery.

ZIMBABWE The windowless tower is probably Africa's most mysterious single structure. It is solid masonry. There is no way to get to the top. What was its purpose?

**MOHENJO-DARO** The earliest Indus Valley civilization, Mohenjo-Daro emerged full grown dating back to 3000 B.C. The cit was planned in detail before it was built.
—Embassy of Pakistan

There was a very sophisticated aquaduct and plumbing system. The Great Baths were probably for religious or ceremonial bathings. — Embassy of Pakistan

**JERICHO** Jericho is the oldest walled town known to archaeology. It was built with great boulders with a 30-foot watchtower. Could Joshuha's trumpet tumble such a wall?

# 9

# Britain's Shadow People

It was the half-dark before daybreak in June, four or five thousand years ago, in the Wiltshire uplands of England. Torches were pale in the growing light. Gazing back through the murk of time, I had glimpses of a procession along an avenue of stone—of priests, perhaps fantastically arrayed in skins and horns and fearsome painted masks, of chiefs with necklaces of teeth, their great heads of hair held up with pins of bone, of women in skins or flaxen robes, of a great peering crowd of shock-headed men and naked children.

They had come from distant places for this one dawn alone. The plain around was dotted with encampments, but the camps were deserted; everyone had left them for the bonfires, for the winding procession with torches around the fields, and at last the climax of this annual festival of the New Year.

Now there was chanting, I thought, or offering of sacrifices. The god alone stood silent, barely visible at the altar in the gloom of the shrine. Priests called invocations. Then the worshipers' eyes, sensitized by the dimness, saw the god suddenly shine between dark shadows as the sun's first beam shone straight at him down the long alley of roughhewn temple pillars.

At least this was how it seemed to me—and to students of the remarkable fact of "orientation" in the megalithic monuments of ancient civilizations and tribes.

Many temples of Egypt and Babylonia were meticulously oriented—that is, built so that all grand entries faced the same direction. In Babylon this was due east, where the sun would rise on March 21 and September 21, the equinoxes. The spring equinox, at least, was important because it was then that the Euphrates and the Tigris flooded.

The pyramids at Giza were also oriented east and west. The Sphinx faced east. However, many Egyptian temples south of the Nile delta faced the point where the sun rose on the longest day, or where the star Sirius shone on that same dawn—for in Egypt the Nile's annual rise occurred close to that date.

Greek temples and theaters were oriented for optimum light or shadow during the year. I wondered how they had accomplished this, because it was illegal to study the sun's movements (it was considered sacrilegious) in Athens at the height of the Periclean age. The Altar of Heaven in Peking was oriented to midwinter, and one of the Chinese emperor's most important duties was to spend midwinter's day in this temple, sacrificing and praying for a propitious year.

Primitive peoples also understood orientation, seemingly. Far before any cities were known in northwestern Europe—even before the Egyptians built pyramids—a group known to prehistorians as the Megalithic ("Big Stone") Cult was erecting odd and varied monuments of huge rough-cut stones. In our time, many of these were discovered to be exactly oriented to the summer solstice.

These gigantic jumbles lay along the coasts of

Spain and Portugal and deep into France, and in Holland, northern Germany, and much of Scandinavia. But the largest numbers were in and around the British Isles; at least six hundred massive stone shrines still dot the landscape in the uplands from the southern coast of Brittany to the north of Scotland and the Outer Hebrides.

It was 1963 when archaeologists became aware of a purpose in the stone circles of England and Brittany. Some of these circles had been planned, evidently, for the dramatic effect on whoever gathered to watch at dawn on June 24, the first day of summer (called, confusingly, Midsummer's Day in Europe). At dawn of that one day, a priest could stand at the altar in the exact center and be irradiated with glory when the rising sun shone directly at him, like a theater spotlight, through a line of stone pillars or squared portals. Who could doubt that these carefully engineered stone calendars were also meant to be places of worship?

All evidence seems to show that most were built around 2000 B.C., when presumably there were only farmers and herdsmen thereabouts. Could there have been a large organized religion as well?

Some of the monuments in Europe dated back as far as 3500 B.C., but others were as recent as 1500 B.C. Most seemed to be simply huge gravestones or memorials. But even these might yet turn out to be extremely significant in some way, as had the stone circles and avenues in England.

Man's desire to worship heavenly bodies seems to have been part of his story since he first began to think about past and future, which were an extremely important part of his life. He had to anticipate seasons in order to survive, especially in intemperate parts of the world. Long before he conceived of numbers and learned to count days or moons, he was wondering "When?" When would the migrating deer pass his hills? When should he prepare cold-weather shelter? When would the highest tides come, and the lowest? When should he plant?

He could reckon seasons from the most noticeable heavenly body. The annual turning point in the sun's course was the summer solstice. After climbing higher day by day, the luminary turned and retraced its course.

Primitive man must have puzzled over this phenomenon when he began to observe the paths of the great lights across the sky. Remembering—but not understanding—the harsh cyclic changes of nature, which seemed to be connected with the long rhythm of the sun's changing habits, perhaps he fancied that rites could magically persuade the sun to stay longer, or could rekindle the sinking flame of the red lamp.

Whatever their origin, "midsummer" rites took place through a quarter of the world from Ireland on the west to Russia on the east, from Norway and Sweden on the north to Spain and Greece on the south. Early folk tales and written records mentioned them as having been celebrated since time immemorial.

They weren't originally celebrated in great stone rings, of course. The first festivals must have been bonfires and torch processions. Only when someone began to mark the sun's movements did the idea arise of placing big stones in certain patterns so that someone who knew how could foretell the day when the sun would make its highest and longest arc. Having invented this, designers might have thought of using the same stone reckoning-circles as temples where the ignorant could be summoned periodically to pray and be impressed.

Of all these places the largest and most awesome were in England, Scotland, Ireland, and Brittany. Greatest of all was a pattern of gigantic stone structures standing alone on the broad Salisbury Plain in southern England. Its original name is unknown, but the name that came down from post-Roman times is Stonehenge, which meant "stones hanging" in the old Anglo-Saxon.

Stonehenge was laid out in a definite but mysterious pattern. Around the site was a circular ditch a hundred yards in diameter. Inside it, great stones (some tumbled or broken in recent centuries) had stood in four series. The two outermost series formed circles. The third was a horseshoe. The innermost was an oval enclosing a central block of blue marble, sixteen feet long by four across, known as the Altar Stone.

The outermost circular colonnade consisted of upright eighteen-foot sandstone pillars, connected by horizontal slabs atop them—the "hanging" stones. These weren't merely resting on top. Someone had cut perfectly round holes in them, which fitted exactly onto projections from the flat tops of the uprights. (I had seen this same peg-and-hole plan in the great gate at Mycenae.) Moreover, the capstones were locked together laterally, with tongue-and-groove joints. Somebody had to lift them twenty feet, then fit them precisely into place like a gigantic Chinese puzzle. They were leveled so accurately that I wondered how it could have been done without instruments.

The two tallest stones (twenty-two feet) were in the middle of the horseshoe, with a fifteen-foot capstone over them. Outside the circle to the northeast stood another pair of stones—and beyond that, one great slab called the Friar's Heel. Once a year someone could stand at the Altar Stone, peer through the pillars of the two great circles and the pair of outer stones, and see the rising sun just above the heel stone.

This fact was forgotten with the passing of centuries. Natives made up more exotic explanations for Stonehenge and other huge prehistoric monuments like Avebury twenty miles to the north, Castle Rigg in Scotland, the "giants' graves" of Newgrange within the Bend of the Boyne in Ireland, and the great South Brittany monolith (now broken in three pieces), which once towered more than sixty feet high, was clearly visible ten miles across the sea, and was estimated to weigh 680,000 pounds.

Avebury was as strange as Stonehenge but in slightly different fashion. Its outermost stone circle was so immense that a village later stood inside it. Two other circles, precisely concentric, were within. Villagers broke up most of Avebury, thinking it was a home of evil spirits, around 1300 A.D., but in recent times some hundred stones were put back.

Very different was nearby Silbury Hill. It was an

imposing man-made mount 130 feet high, containing more than twelve million cubic feet of turf and chalk rubble—the biggest artificial hill in Europe. It was carefully built up in a series of layers, with great insight into problems of soil engineering. The sides were carefully terraced. Radial walls of chalk inside the hill added stability. But its purpose remains unknown.

Everyone agrees that these monuments had to have been of supernatural origin. No mortal could have fixed such masses in such precise symmetry. Obviously they belonged to the remote past, when giants and heroes and wizards walked the land. The Celts of Brittany, Wales, and Ireland named their prehistoric stone formations in accordance with the known fact that the "little people" could lift any amount of weight. The English, harking back to tales of Druid priests, attributed Stonehenge and other stone rings to them. Or, some thought, King Arthur and his knights might be responsible.

What was England really like, I wondered, in its earliest days of human habitation? Who among its inhabitants might have built Stonehenge?

Originally the island was part of the European mainland. There was a land bridge between the future Dover and Calais. Across that low tidewater plain walked primitive hunters, following the last receding ice sheet in pursuit of mammoth and reindeer. Later—since England was so accessible then—came invaders, whether in peace or war, as pirate or merchant, conqueror or missionary.

In the impenetrable fog of millennia, vague shapes of men moved: men of the Old Stone Age, and the New Stone Age, and newcomers from the Rhine with bronze tools and bell-shaped pottery cups. Maybe one of these craftsmen stood on a chalk hill, pointed to the valley at his feet, and said to his grandson, "The sea comes farther up that inlet than it did when I was a boy." The grandson might have lived to see a high tide go roaring all the way through the valley, scouring out its sides, joining the North Sea with the Channel.

After that, little clans no longer waded across in search of game or tasty plants. There were no more quick dashes in dugout canoes or wicker coracles through narrow inlets at ebb tide. Those who came had to come in ships, and had to be bold and shrewd sailors to survive in the winds and tides of the Channel. The island began to be different.

When did this tremendous severing occur? Geologists used to assign it to periods before Neolithic man. But the study of striped clays and glacial deposits, and other indications, gave a tolerably accurate chart of many thousands of years. Trawlers brought up fragments of trees in their nets—proof that less than nine thousand years ago oaks were growing where stormy water is now sixty fathoms deep.

After the tide race widened into the Straits of Dover, and then after twenty or thirty generations of the spreading use of bronze, what were the primitive Englishmen like? Professor R. C. Collingwood drew a detailed picture:

> Britain was backward by comparison with the Continent; primitive in its civilization, stagnant and passive in its life, receiving most of what progress it enjoyed through invasion and importation from overseas.
>
> Its people lived in isolated farms or hut-villages . . . by agriculture and livestock, augmented no doubt by hunting and fishing. They made rude pottery without a wheel, but they were visited by itinerant bronze-founders able to make swords, axes, sickles, carpenters tools, metal parts of wheeled vehicles, buckets, and cauldrons.
>
> Judging by the absence of towns, these people were little organized, and their political life was simple and undeveloped.

This late Bronze Age in the island, by all evidence, began about 1000 B.C. and lasted until about 400 B.C. But the Romans, when they came in 55 B.C. to colonize Britain, found no written language there.

But for Stonehenge the radiocarbon date estimated for the beginning of construction was between 2775 and

1900 B.C. Construction may have continued until as late as 1400 B.C. So we must assume that those who planned and built it were Stone Age types—even less skillful than their ignorant Bronze Age successors described by Professor Collingwood!

And so the most celebrated monument surviving from pre-Roman England loomed as a huge, silent contradiction to everything archaeologists and geologists had deduced about the island.

The stark fact seems to be that a large number of people, for some almost unimaginable reason, felt a compulsion to transport at least eighty stones, weighing four tons or more apiece, from Mount Prescelly in southwestern Wales (definitely identified as the source of the Stonehenge rock) to Salisbury Plain—135 miles as the crow flies.

Oh, primitives could do it, theoretically.

They could quarry and shape the rock by chipping with stones, a millimeter at a time. The biggest slab, weighing fifty tons (half again as much as the heaviest "juggernaut" truck now allowed to travel freely on highways); could be moved on sledge and rollers by fifteen hundred men. Given time enough, they could drag and push it to the Bristol Channel. Next they could build an enormous raft to transport it by sea and thence by rivers—with occasional overland portages—to within two miles of the plain. And in a few additional years, perhaps, they could move the other megaliths too.

Could have? *Must* have.

Unless they knew a way to make giant stones travel through the air.

But what was the point of their stupendous feat? At that early date, why did they determine to worship gods in a circle of stones rather than in simpler structures better suited to the times? Who procured and distributed the necessary food to keep the laborers alive during the millions of man-days devoted to the job? What inducements enlisted carpenters, weavers, hunters, and others needed to accompany such a big task force?

The main phase of the building alone must have taken a thousand-man force some ten years to complete, according to construction experts. Yet they were living in a subsistence economy, when most people needed to work from dawn to dark merely to scratch a living.

In trying to reconcile the megalithic structures with the archaeological insistence that the builders were illiterate farmers, experts showed ingenuity in inventing methods by which the stones could have been erected without tools or apparatus beyond what the primitives might have had. Experiments showed that such methods were feasible.

Yet I wondered—did the scientists who figured out these procedures design them entirely in their heads, without pencil or paper? Did everyone work from oral instructions only—no charts, no specifications, no pictures or written descriptions?

An organizational genius would be needed, I thought, to coordinate a thousand men by word-of-mouth alone.

To me, the question wasn't whether intelligent, civilized men with Stone Age tools could do the job. The question was whether Stone Age men—illiterate, hindered by superstitions, untrained—were capable first of conceiving the complex structure of Stonehenge, second of planning it in detail without drawings, and finally of organizing for the prolonged and herculean toil needed to cut and move the stones and set them up on the site.

The only imaginable answer, to me, was that some other people, much more civilized, also lived in Britain during the thousand-odd-year period when Stonehenge and other astronomically aligned megaliths were being built. In historic times, two peoples with different racial origins and different levels of culture often lived side by side. Surely it could happen in a prehistoric age too.

Wouldn't the more advanced race leave traces of itself? Perhaps it had. Recently, British archaeologists began studying what they called a "Wessex culture," which existed around 1550 B.C. The only evidence I knew about was in 130 mound graves. But all were graves of aristocrats, with fine bronze pins from central Europe; gold earrings presumably from Ireland, where the nearest gold lay; fine pottery from Brittany; amber drinking cups and magnificent necklaces with several hundred amber beads, of unknown origin. One mound in Cornwall contained a goldsmith's masterpiece: a cup hammered from a single sheet of gold, its handle attached by gold rivets and washers.

Then too, tombs were being excavated within sight of Stonehenge itself. They were comparable to those of Mycenae. For example, a man entombed in an eleven-foot-high burial mound had a solid gold breastplate as big as a dinner plate. He wore a belt with a two-piece gold clasp, beautifully worked. Three bronze daggers were with him, and the handle of one was designed in chevrons with thousands of tiny gold pins. A bronze ax was wrapped in cloth. Bronze rivets above the skull suggested a helmet.

Whoever these unknown elite were, they disappeared completely by the time the Roman Empire grew interested in Britain. Small numbers of them might have inhabited the country for one or two thousand years, building colossal stone observatories and using them, perhaps while the kings of Minoan Crete and Mycenaean Greece came and went. Then their miniature civilization quietly passed away, for uncertain reasons.

While it lasted, it was more subtle and sophisticated than anyone guessed until recently. In the 1960s, astronomers turned their eyes on Stonehenge and other megaliths. Professor Alexander Thom of Oxford surveyed some six hundred sites over the area from the Orkney Islands and Outer Hebrides to the south of Brittany. His findings were almost incredible.

He discovered that the builders worked with a standard unit of measurement at all their many sites over a period of centuries. The unit never varied: always 32.64 inches, or 829 millimeters. (Another investigator, C. A. Newham, found the same unit used in Greece's Parthenon.)

Thom also noticed that certain sites were laid out not in circles but in enormous ellipses with the perimeter exactly three times larger than the largest diameter. This trick could only be done with complex theorems based on Pythagorean triangles. Why bother? Because the moon swings around the earth in an elliptical orbit, and sightings from the center of the stone oval could measure slow oscillations of the moon's orbit.

Somebody in the Stone Age was far ahead of all astronomers of whom we have record. Our civilization didn't detect that the moon bobbed and weaved slightly on the horizon, because of the sun's varying pull, until the sixteenth century A.D.

Strangest of all, Thom said, in northernmost Scotland and at Carnac in Brittany were tapering grids of massive stones that could be used as computers for solving quadratic equations. By lining up the sun and moon with various stones, a mathematician could predict certain important positions—such as the precise dates on which eclipses would occur.

Thom's explanations of the fan-shaped patterns, and of three thousand standing stones in avenues at Carnac, are so complicated that they cannot be understood by the average reader. But they were clear to Professor Fred Hoyle of Cambridge. He verified and applauded them while other savants derided them as "moonshine."

He also got busy analyzing the majestic geometry of Stonehenge.

There he found that "alignments are just the ones that could have served far-reaching astronomical purposes." Standing among the giant slabs, looking through one of the narrow stone portals and an aligned portal in the outer ring, he felt that his field of view was tightly controlled, as by sighting instruments, so that he couldn't avoid seeing the rising or setting of celestial bodies on certain key dates.

There were 120 pairs of such positions. One showed the two extreme positions of midwinter moonrise, when the moon rode across the sky at its highest. Another marked an orbital cycle of eighteen and a half years. Stonehenge was locked to the sun and moon as tightly as are the tides. It was an astronomical observatory and a fifty-six-year calendar.

Hoyle had asked himself: "If we twentieth-century people with our brains and knowledge, but without modern equipment, set out to do what the builders of Stonehenge apparently succeeded in doing, how would we set about it?"

He took into consideration the sidereal month, 27⅓ days; the synodic month, 29½ days; the variations in time of moonrise from one night to the next, which average about fifty minutes but dwindle to almost nothing for several nights during the time of the harvest moon in northern climes; the cycle between nearly similar solar eclipses of eighteen years plus eleven or ten days according to the occurrence of leap years; and a host of other recurring intervals.

To answer his rigorously complicated question, he imagined himself on another planet where orbits of sun and moon were different. How would he plot the movements of that solar system using only sticks and stones and string? The answer, he concluded, was to make a pattern like Stonehenge.

His reasoning was deeply technical. It included twenty-eight equations. To me this made his argument unconvincing at first. The more complicated the mathematics, the less likely that Stone Age people used them.

Hoyle's reply was that his theory "not only requires Stonehenge to have been constructed as an astronomical instrument but demands a level of intellectual attainment orders of magnitude higher than the standard to be expected from a community of primitive farmers. A veritable Newton or Einstein must have been at work. But then, why not?"

Most of the megaliths were clustered in an area across which a man could walk in four months. But even those lying much farther apart showed so many identical features that they must have come from a "megalithic religion," or at least a megalithic tradition, branching from Cyprus to Sweden by way of Spain, and extending over a period of more than two thousand years. Was a completely unrecorded, unsuspected brotherhood at work?

Designers of megaliths must have understood how the cycles of eclipses were determined. They could have worked this out only if they'd been recording the dates for centuries. But why pursue such work in Britain?

Many eclipses weren't observable there, either because of bad weather or because of geographic location. When visible, they wouldn't be as impressive to sun worshipers or moon worshipers as they would be in brighter regions.

One of the few factors that made Britain a good place for sky study, so far as I knew, was that the horizon in northern latitudes would give a good sight line for the apparent slow weaving of the moon. This deviation, which at its maximum appeared as only about two thirds of the width of the sun, could be seen at the maximum in Britain.

Not being sociologists or anthropologists or historians, Thom and Hoyle made no conjecture as to why people on this far northern island would be curious about eclipse dates and other meteorological cycles. Satisfaction of their curiosity required the immense toil of stone moving as well as elaborate record keeping and calculating. Again I asked myself, Why did they bother?

Maybe because they were providing the information for people who badly needed it elsewhere.

In a theocracy like Egypt or Sumer, or perhaps Crete or Mycenae, priest-rulers could use such data to enhance their power. They could do much more than tell their flock when to plant and harvest, and be proven right. On the day or night that a faraway stone computer had predicted an eclipse, they might well give dire warnings, somewhat as the Connecticut Yankee did at Camelot in Mark Twain's fantasy. And when the prophesied blotting out of the heavenly body started, they could intone the magic words that enabled the sun or the moon to escape the blackness.

Maybe they couldn't build the necessary massive stone patterns in their own land, for reasons of latitude or topography, or simply because their people would have asked too many questions. Very well. Suppose they sent expeditions to England and Wales and Brittany to arrange for construction and observation. Then how did they keep in touch through the centuries? Were they capable of telepathy or teleportation, as Hindu sages were said to be?

Probably no one will ever know. But I thought I knew what eventually happened to the unknown elite.

Men armed with iron arrived and slaughtered the men of bronze. At this point we could recognize across the millennia a fellow being. A creature capable of killing someone with iron was surely, to modern eyes, a man and a brother. It took brains to know that iron was better than bronze for bashing skulls.

England's transition from Bronze Age to Iron Age took a long time. Bronze was still used widely until the last century before Christ. Collingwood wrote:

> Many settlements indicate a mode of life not perceptibly different from that of their late Bronze Age background; they are farms or villages, often undefended, still using bronze and even flint implements and possessing very little iron, but indicating their date by a change in the style of their pottery.

This was about three centuries before Christ. But as the newcomers with iron weapons multiplied and developed, local wars erupted. The country grew more savage. Belgic tribes, a people of chariots and horsemen, arrived and built fortified towns. But the tramp of the legions was following them.

In Rome, at the center and summit, the western island was perceived only hazily. It was thought to be a subdivision of Hades where ghosts floated in half-light, crying with weird voices of sea birds. But on the frontier, Julius Caesar had more explicit information. Here are impressions he collected before crossing the Channel:

> The interior of Britain is inhabited by people who claim, on the strength of oral tradition, to be aboriginal; the coast, by Belgic immigrants who came to plunder and make war. . . . All Britons dye their bodies with woad, which produces a blue color, and gives them a more terrifying appearance in battle. They wear their hair long, and shave the whole of their bodies except the head and upper lip.

The Romans hated and feared the sea. In a supreme effort at survival they had put down the Etruscan pirates and surpassed Carthage in its own element in the Mediterranean. But the idea of Roman legions landing in the remote, unknown, gloomy island of the north was strange and thrilling to all ranks of Roman society.

In the end, Rome gave the word and the legions sailed. Caesar saw the Britons as a tougher and cruder branch of the Celtics he had faced in Gaul and had never forgotten. Those whom he fought in Britain were just as fearsome. Not only did they paint themselves blue, they drove war chariots hooked with scythes at the axles.

Their religion was that of the Druids, with terrible white-robed priests who were said to drive a man mad by throwing a wisp of straw in his face. Druids had profoundly influenced the life of Germany and Gaul as well as Britain. "Those who want to study Druidism," wrote Caesar, "generally go to Britain for the purpose."

Romans (and later peoples) knew little about Druid beliefs except that they undoubtedly entailed human sacrifice. The mysterious priesthoods of the trees bound themselves and their votaries by the most deadly sacraments that men could take. Although Romans had scant respect for human life, as everyone knew from their treatment of gladiators and Christians, they drew the line at murder to please the gods. Caesar and the proconsuls worked systematically to drive Druids out of England. Some found refuge in the Welsh mountains. There, for perhaps another thousand years, their descendants kept alive under the name Merlin (from the Celtic sky god Myrddhin) the tradition of magic that had been handed down since the unknown time when the Druids came out of nowhere—or perhaps out of Africa, as one legend said.

I talked with Gerald Hawkins, author of *Beyond Stonehenge,* and asked if he would speculate about the origin of the people who created the arches of Stonehenge. Could they be, I wondered, other-worldly? I have long fancied the notion that some of humanity's progress on the planet Earth is traceable to influences of extraterrestrials. Dr. Hawkins refused to elaborate on my speculative thrust. I settled for a description of the capabilities that the builders of Stonehenge must have possessed. I asked Dr. Hawkins what it took to build Stonehenge.

"I estimate one and a half million man days of work and many broken legs," he replied. "Certainly the stones couldn't be carried but they would have to be rolled or dragged. One archeologist has called them howling barbarians, but I prefer to regard them not as primitive people but simple people in their lifestyle. I believe that a lot of their thought processes exist with us today and a lot of their achievements are what we're striving for. As to what was in their minds, I have uncovered certain very hard facts, numerical relationships, an interest in precision, an interest in time patterns and this means something very fundamental to the psychological basis to their beliefs. What they were doing was a complete entity to them, and it must have been extremely satisfying. They did not do it by being driven as slaves. They did not do it for money because there was no monetary system. They did it because they wanted to, and here we have perhaps the beginning of our civilization, the essence of civilization, a community with a common purpose and a common set of ideas."

Britain was a Roman province for nearly four hundred years, most of which were tranquil and left little for history to note. The Romans built noble roads, fortresses, market cities, country houses—whose ruins the next comers contemplated with awe. But Roman law, language, and institutions disappeared when the legions left the province to sink or swim in the great convulsion of the Dark Ages.

A strange fact emerged many centuries later when scholars pored through the detailed reports by Roman officials in Britain. Nowhere did they mention Stonehenge or other strange megaliths. Surely the Romans, as great builders themselves, were puzzled by the huge stone circles. Why were they silent?

Perhaps they loathed Druids too much to mention

any works, as they thought, of the occult practitioners. Stonehenge had probably become notorious as a Druid temple. By the seventeenth century all such "rude monuments" were commonly ascribed to the last pre-Christian inhabitants of each country—in Scandinavia to the Vikings, in France to the Gauls, and in Britain to the Celts and especially their Celtic priests and judges and seers, the Druids.

Even in my own travels I had heard people damn Stonehenge as a bloody place where Druids read the omens, sacrificed humans, and who knew what else. But even if Stonehenge was used for Druid rites, it was not built by Druids. Archaeologists proved decades ago that Stonehenge was twice as old as the Druids. Even so, right up to today, members of a "Most Ancient Order of Druids" meet at Stonehenge and perform secret ceremonies that they say date back to Atlantis.

In medieval times people got another wild idea that could account for Roman silence about Stonehenge, if the idea were somehow true. Geoffrey of Monmouth (found later to be a fanciful fellow who confused facts with myth) wrote in the twelfth century that Merlin the great magician had whisked the stones to Salisbury from Ireland, where they first had been set up by giants "from the remotest confines of Africa."

Merlin? The dread wizard of King Arthur's time?

King Arthur, whoever he was, might have known Stonehenge but assuredly had nothing to do with building it. Still, he was another British wraith who intrigued me. I went to see the places where he might have left some ghostly aura.

Countless generations had searched before me. A Welsh bard, it was told, searched all new-made graves throughout the land, beneath the trees of the forests, down in the valleys, and along by the gray sea; but no stone was marked for Arthur. Then his muse awoke and told him, "What folly it would be to think that Arthur had a grave—that kingly one, always with gentle words for the oppressed, and a sharp edge for the ruffian, and a spirit that put a blessing everywhere. He died in battle and the black queens took him in a barge across torch-lit water and he was never seen again."

This I could understand. But what had the cold-blooded researchers learned?

The roots of the Arthurian saga stretched far back to the long night of 400–600 A.D. when barbarian invaders were driving Britons to seek safety in the Welsh hills or across the Channel in the part of France that became known as Brittany. These emigrés told of a sublime leader fighting to save them. After 1066 when the Normans came through Brittany and conquered England, the old tales of an Arthur were picked up and embroidered into epic verse by French poets—followed by Malory, Spenser, Tennyson, T. H. White, and many others.

So the Arthur behind the legends probably led his riders in decades when murderous tribes were seeping into the vacuum left after the legions went home to guard their doomed capital. The little Picts scampered over the abandoned Hadrian's Wall in the north; Scotti tribes (later to be called Irish) harried the coasts from their camps in northern Ireland. The unsubdued Celts came from Wales, hearty Jutes from Jutland in Denmark, businesslike Angles from Angeln in Schleswig. The Saxons rowed in longboats from the coast of Germany to ravage the eastern shores and—finding the pickings good—to settle permanently.

Of all the Teutonic tribes none was more cruel than the Saxons. They took their tribal name, which spread to the whole miscellany of northern raiders, from their word *seaxan,* which meant "user of a short sword." Once a collector let me handle a seax. There are times when I have a peculiar sensitivity to objects associated with violent happenings, and this was one of them. As I closed my hand on the pommel I was shaken by a sensation of utter brutal strength, truculence, and power. I saw a stocky towheaded man with a bursting gorge who cared for nothing that walked on two legs. I seemed to feel him so electrically that I put the weapon away.

About a century after the Romans left, Saxons and Angles battered their way through half of what would later be called Angle-land: England. But their advance was slowing, because the timid natives had begun to dash out from their stone-walled sheepfolds and hit back vigorously.

The Saxons were infantry, fighting close in with sword and spear, wearing little armor. But the day of infantry had passed for a time, and the day of the legions had passed forever. Cavalry were on the rise. Disciplined swordsmen and spearmen wearing chain mail, riding horses, protected by iron scales sewn through blankets, could slash into mobs of Saxon foot fighters with terrible effect. Apparently Arthur and his "knights" were a band of such horsemen, ranging across the three-hundred-mile width of Britain wherever danger threatened, rallying local resistance and winning repeated victories.

Twelve battles, all at places now unknown, were celebrated in the Latin of a Welsh chronicler, Nennius, who completed his *Historia Britonum* less than two centuries after the events it described. He named the general of the British forces, victorious in all twelve clashes, as a certain Artorius.

The twelfth victory, Nennius wrote, "was on Mount Badon, where in one day nine hundred and sixty men fell in one charge of Arthur's." The victory was so devastating that it brought the Saxons to a standstill for almost forty years.

Gildas, a sixth-century monk who probably was writing only a few years after Arthur's death, and may even have known him, also hailed the crowning triumph at Mount Badon—with not a word of Arthur. This mysterious omission led some later historians to believe that no such "Arthur" existed. But Gildas might have had reasons of his own not to name him.

Perhaps Arthur, like so many of his contemporaries, fell short of the monk's strict ideals in religion or morals, so Gildas broke with him. Gildas hinted at this elsewhere. Or possibly there were personal reasons for the quarrel, if quarrel there was. According to a biography of Gildas written centuries later in the abbey where Gildas had lived, an elder brother named Hueil made some traitorous bargain with Pict marauders, and Arthur fought him and killed him. If this actually happened, I could understand Gildas's refusal to perpetuate the name of his enemy. But he did refer to a British leader whom he called The Bear. The Celtic word for "bear" was *arth* or *artos*.

The peace that Arthur won for his countrymen was not so long for him. Twenty years after Badon, various followers turned against him—perhaps incited by his illegitimate son Mordred, as described by bards—and wounded him. He was borne away to a certain unknown Isle of Avalon, "hidden in mist and mysterious waters," where he died.

Some legends said that he and his lady Guinevere were buried in Glastonbury Abbey. The good monks there felt sure that this was true. And in 1911, when they needed funds to restore their burnt-out buildings, they made a timely discovery of what they said were Arthur's bones. These were reverently interred in a new and more magnificent abbey, only to be lost with everything else when Henry VIII dissolved all monasteries.

This is all that history knows of the supposed King Arthur, guardian of the Holy Grail. And even this was written from hearsay. We have no solid proof that he existed. But it is an interesting fact that Arthur as a Christian name for boys became popular in the sixth century, whereas it had been rare before.

Lately some fascinating evidence was dug up by archaeologists. In southwest England they found remains of an Iron Age fortress that Leslie Alcock of the University College of South Wales, in charge of the excavations, called "the most exciting thing I've seen in all my archaeological experience." Dr. Ralegh Radford, an expert on early Christian archaeology, said the find supported "the traditional identification of the site as the Camelot of Arthurian legend."

Even to my amateur eye the hill that loomed above the quiet village of South Cadbury seemed like a proper perch for a warrior chieftain. It appeared to be an immense artificial mound, rising steeply in waves of banks and ditches. I climbed to the summit, which was flat and grassy—and spacious enough for a royal castle. It extended for eighteen acres.

From that commanding martial height I could envision, instead of the near field below, misty swamps that once were in their place. Arthur could surely have galloped out across the causeway (still faintly marked through the farmland) to meet the foe. It was an evocative place.

Digging was still going on. A young volunteer, one of many student excavators, said that each morning he felt excited; one day, he was sure, he or a colleague would brush away dirt from dramatic proof that Arthur had truly ruled there.

I was told that local people had known the place as Camelot at least since the time of Henry VIII. Two nearby villages were still called West Camel and Queen Camel. (England had no camels, of course.) Villagers said that ghostly horses clattered through the towns on quiet nights.

However that might be, there is proof that this was already a hill fortress when the Romans came. Its Briton defenders were put to the sword by legionaries. And it was refortified in the sixth century as a stronghold against the barbarians. There were enough shards of fine red jars, called Tintagel ware, imported from the Mediterranean area by sixth-century Britons of wealth and position, to suggest that a princely warrior dwelt there. More recently, diggers unearthed part of a foundation trench for what seemed to be a large hall cut into the bedrock of the plateau. Such a room, sixty feet by thirty, might be the great hall of Camelot. Or might not.

Professor Alcock said that only one seven-hundredth of the interior was exposed so far. Funds were inadequate for large-scale excavation. I hoped that the work could go faster soon.

Meanwhile, there was also excitement at Glastonbury Tor, rising from a waterlogged plain twelve miles to the northwest. Local lore had long identified it as the Isle of Avalon, and now evidence was being found. This place too was a towering hill—but a completely natural one, unlike the site of Cadbury Castle. It could well have been a signaling station for Arthur's cavalry, because it was clearly visible from Cadbury. Brent Knoll and Dinas Powys—other high hills in the vicinity—gave visibility for forty miles. Via those heights,

British defenders could have kept in touch from Wales to Cadbury.

Glastonbury was once an island—a fortified lake village of huts on massive logs pile-driven into the waterlogged peat. Before Arthur's time the island was the site of a wattle church, said to be the first Christian church in England. It grew into the great Benedictine monastery (second only to Westminster Abbey) where Arthur's bones were assertedly found. Now the digging was turning up bits of sixth-century treasure. This seemed to indicate that some very important person had dwelt with the black-robed monks. Who more likely than Arthur?

And then there were the tumbled walls of Tintagel Castle, on a narrow neck of rock across a chasm on the Cornwall coast. The baby Arthur was born there and handed over to Merlin's care, legends said. Other legends had it that this was Camelot, for when the Duke of Cornwall lived there it was called Camelford.

It looked to be a place where Arthur's ghost might linger. The dark stone of the ruined gables stood stark against an ever-changing sky, magically pinkish-orange turning to dull leaden gray and then to royal purple. The air was damp, and crashing waves echoed hollowly.

Yet the old "castle" whose remnants I saw was never Arthur's haunt; this was a Norman chapel built long after his time. On the other hand, the foundations of a sixth-century Celtic monastery also lay hereabouts. The place had a brooding sense of mystery and fantasy. Anything could have happened here.

I fancied I saw the Once and Future King. But he was not in medieval panoply as story books showed him. Shiny armor was unknown in his century. I saw a rough young captain riding out, fingers on the ashen shaft of a tall spear tipped with polished iron. Instead of armor he wore a loose glimmery gown of chain mail. He had no plumed helmet, but a nut-shaped iron headpiece lined with leather. A heavy iron sword in a leather scabbard swung from his high padded saddle. His boots were dull leather, his legs trousered in coarse muslin. His wool cloak was fastened at the shoulder with a gleaming bronze brooch.

This leathery fighter rode through dark, unspecified times. The places of his battles might never be found. But I could believe that someone like him had kept the light of civilization burning against all the storms that beat. When he and his faithful had ridden down to death, and England became Anglo-Saxon despite them, they left behind the large, uncertain, dim but glittering legend that would perennially awaken something hidden in the hearts of all heroic men.

# 10

# Egypt's Black Rival

When I began my quest for lost civilizations I hadn't expected to look deep into Africa. But in Crete, in Mycenae, in the Bible and other classical writings, and even in prehistoric Britain, I'd seen clues pointing in that direction. So I took a plane and followed the clues.

First I wanted to see ancient Nubia. Reaching it took a long time.

Flying south, the horizon unrolling evenly ahead like a blue ripple over a still blue sea, I marveled at the terrifying emptiness of the continent. Africa was a land of lost trails, lost people, lost cities, lost treasures, lost aircraft. Along stretches of coast I saw lost ships.

When I was a boy I once asked, "Why is it called the Dark Continent?" The answer, as I recall, was that Africa was an immense unknown, a dark place in the mind of man. Africans were strangely unlike other people. Their origin was a mystery. The interior of their continent was suffused with legends of witch doctors, secret societies, jujus, and mumbo-jumbo.

Almost until the other day our race commonly held that African folkways were products of ignorance. Blacks seemingly belonged to the beginnings, with no inherited records or knowledge. Everything in Africa was frozen in primal bliss and horror. A British governor of Nigeria summed up our belief: "For countless centuries, while all the pageant of history swept by, the African remained unmoved—in primitive savagery."

It never occurred to us, from the seventeenth century until almost the middle of the twentieth, that turning a blind eye toward African culture had been a way of rationalizing the slave trade and more recent cruelties. We didn't know that early explorers had found Africans to be far from ignorant. We were content with the "scientific" verdict of the famed nineteenth-century naturalist Louis Agassiz that Africans "never originated a regular organization among themselves."

But a time came when the hidden faces behind ancient African masks were seen differently. They might still look strange and savage, but the word *primitive* wasn't altogether correct. Black civilizations had been making history in their own ways for a very long time. Their drama in its early acts was invisible to the Western world—but the cast was stellar, the action forceful, and the settings often surprisingly artistic.

I could understand why the New World and Australia had been unvisited for so long. Europe at that time did not know of their existence. But Africa was different. The world's second-largest continent lay for thousands of years in full view of venturesome civilizations that came and went around the Aegean and the Mediterranean. It was a known unknown, a dark secret in the staring sun. It stayed mostly unfathomed until our own restless civilization pushed toward its heart.

Why had Africa lain unvisited for so long? I studied maps, and saw why.

The answer wasn't just indifference among Mediterranean peoples, nor their tendency to double back toward the glittering East. The interior of sub-Saharan Africa was armed by nature to fend off visitors.

The blazing Sahara sealed the north. Eastern flanks were guarded by parched Red Sea hills, unfriendly Ethiopia's mountain vastnesses, and the enormous swamps of the valley of the Nile. More deserts barred the southern edge behind a shore so bleak that it was (and is) known as the Skeleton Coast. Facing the Atlantic, the jungle descended in sullen masses, later described by Winston Churchill as "a glittering equatorial slum [where] huge trees jostle one another for room to live." Rivers weren't navigable for any distance inland. Nearly everywhere hard by the coast, the land rose steeply to a great tilting plateau that stretched thousands of miles.

The barriers weren't impregnable but they seemed so to Europeans, who had to cross seas before they could even examine the coast. For centuries they stayed away. But eventually they drew closer, because Portugal's Prince Henry, whom history entitled Henry the Navigator—although he himself never went to sea—prodded his captains out in search of far shores.

Henry borrowed from the superior technology of Arab sailors to produce caravels that could sail into the wind without the help of galley slaves; and he got scientists to solve problems of navigation, so that captains could plot a course and ascertain their whereabouts.

Fifteenth-century Portuguese explorers came home from Africa with incredible—yet often true—stories. They told of scholarly centers in the desert, commercial cities that rivaled Venice, hidden gold mines guarded by disciplined armies. "The king of Wolof can put into the field about ten thousand horsemen and a hundred thousand foot soldiers," reported Pacheco Pereira on returning from Senegal.

In 1441, Nuno Tristão caused the greatest sensation of all: he brought back twelve African natives.

Europe was familiar with brown-skinned Arabs and Indians, but it knew nothing of really black-skinned peoples. A few blacks had been glimpsed in

Moorish slave markets, but they were thought to be freak mutants. Amazed at the strength and agility of the frightened captives, Europe decided that slaves from Africa would be excellent investments. In the next seven years more than nine hundred African slaves were brought to Portugal, baptized for the "good of their souls," and sold as slaves to plantation owners.

So the rush began. Europe's kings and syndicates sent ships ostensibly to explore and convert, but in reality to get slaves, gold, and ivory. Their crews confirmed and elaborated the tall tales about African cultures, noting what other men forgot soon afterward.

In 1498 Vasco da Gama and his sailors, cruising down Africa's eastern coast, were elated to see comfortable, wealthy towns with four-story stone houses among gardens and orchards. Ashore they met black Muslims who knew more about charts and compasses than they did, and who were sometimes more civilized. The townsmen gently rebuked the seamen for crudenesses but offered them precious stones, making clear that "there was no need to purchase them, as they could be collected in baskets," as Da Gama recorded. He returned four years later as invader and pillager of Zanzibar, Mombasa, Kilwa, and Zeila.

Other explorers, arriving at the mouth of the Congo River, found another flamboyant and complex kingdom. The pomp of its court awed even those who had seen Lisbon's royalty. One traveler wrote:

> The king of Congo, when he goeth to the camp to see his army, rideth upon an elephant in great majesty. On either side of the elephant he hath six slaves; two were kings that he himself had taken in the field.
>
> Then there followeth a Moor, which doth nothing but talk aloud in praise of the king, telling what a great warrior he hath been, and praising his wisdom.

The Congo people were not stupid. Another European reported:

> They are a very wary people in their bargaining, and will not lose one spark of gold of any value. They use weights and measures, and are very circumspect.

So the newcomers moved slowly in undoing them. First they persuaded the king of Congo to be baptized a Christian, and then to exchange ambassadors with the Pope and with the Portuguese court. Next they rented land from him. One by one they built trading posts, forts, and bases for expeditions to the interior. This eventually undermined the kingdom. About 1550, tribes from upriver helped the Portuguese overthrow the government—although for decades afterward a Congo king presided in tattered pomp over a small jungle village, the last remnant of the great kingdom.

Similar fates overtook other native nations on both coasts. By 1700 Europe had leaped forward technologically. Africa had not. Disease killed a hundred thousand Africans in Uganda alone. Interior trade networks fell apart. A few fierce states fought off white invaders for centuries, but by 1841, when the great Scottish missionary doctor David Livingstone blazed a trail across the continent, most of the great kingdoms had shrunk to villages, whole cities were gone from the map, and nations and tribes were forgotten or even exterminated.

And so the way was clear for a century of white settlement and colonialism. Sometimes prospectors and immigrants stumbled on strange empty cities of coral and stone in the hothouse darkness of jungles or on ruined fortresses athwart strategic camel trails in the deserts. From Somalia and Ethiopia all the way to sun-seared Transvaal prairies, whites found ghostly mud palaces, prehistoric mine workings, abandoned towns, and carvings and terra-cotta and bronze castings with a wealth of strong styles, some comparable to classical art. Enormous 2,200-year-old stone pyramids were discovered on a once-fertile plain in the Sudan where the Nubian kingdom of Cush had thrived for a thousand years.

So much for the record. The creators of all these works had been swallowed up in time. They left no writings or pictures. Our only clues to them were bits of remembered history here and there, and old reports by travelers.

I knew several young African historians who became the first professors of national history in their new nations. What could they teach? In some African countries the written record began in the nineteenth century. Prehistory in Kenya, for example, meant before 1890!

These young scholars, trained in historiography at Western universities, undertook to compile histories while teaching them. On weekends and vacations they headed for the bush with cameras, notebooks, and tape-recorders. In villages they interviewed the village historians—old men who remembered the village's past, and retold it. They knew the genealogies of local kings, sometimes for thirty generations; the metes and bounds of tribal lands; the chronologies of eclipses and earthquakes. They were roughly equivalent to, so to speak, our county clerks and newspaper files.

All this was in my mind as I skimmed over this land of huge mountains, wide black rivers, and vast spaces of steppe and savanna. I planned to investigate three of Africa's most puzzling civilizations—two long-dead, one still alive. But I kept wondering what had happened earlier, in the many centuries before the Europeans and the slavers came.

I knew of indications that Africa had at odd moments excited the ancients. The Bible mentioned black Africans a dozen times—calling them Ethiopians in the King James version because the original Greek used the word *aithiops,* meaning "burnt faces." The name confused generations of readers because it had no connection with the modern Ethiopia.

More enigmatically, the Old Testament told in I Kings of Solomon's ships returning from a land called Ophir with "gold, silver, ivory and apes," which seemed unlikely to be found anywhere but in Africa. The scripture said that the ships carried more than twelve tons of gold. The same report was repeated almost verbatim in II Chronicles.

Many a scholarly quarrel broke out about this

rich land of Ophir, and many a wanderer sought it. None ever pinpointed it. However, the bulk of the evidence suggested either Somaliland, on the upper eastern coast, or southern Rhodesia.

Twenty-five centuries ago the Phoenician general Hanno sailed down the western coast and brought back gold, as well as strange reports, to his native Carthage in the Mediterranean. A century before him, other Phoenicians apparently steered the other way, down from Suez, and got clear around Africa; this was two thousand years before Da Gama. The Phoenicians' findings led Herodotus, that insatiably curious Greek traveler, to record, "There gold is obtained in great plenty, huge elephants abound, with wild trees of all sorts, and ebony; and the men are taller, handsomer and longer lived than anywhere else." He implied that the Phoenicians traded for their gold among blacks who brought it across a desert from the western coast.

This probably started the trans-Saharan gold trade. It would go on for millennia. The Phoenicians had taken over the old Minoan and Mycenaean sea routes, made themselves the busiest merchants of the ancient world, and probably shipped countless African cargoes to Egypt.

Egypt was well aware of great Negroid nations to its south. Its own frail sailboats couldn't go there. But in its greatest days, when it wasn't insular and rigid, it found other means to make contact with other parts of Africa. It sent donkey trains. Eventually it built bigger vessels and dug a chain of canals to the Red Sea.

Over a period of some centuries, papyrus scrolls and wall inscriptions told of several journeys to a mysterious "land of Punt" (possibly the Somali country near Africa's eastern coast) to procure "sweet-smelling trees of the lands of the gods, incense, ebony, ivory, gold, cosmetics for the eyes, monkeys, panther skins," for which the Egyptians traded beads and baubles.

The Egyptians knew a lot about Punt, which perhaps was the same as the Bible's Ophir. They must have gone there; how else could impressive colored representations of Punt adorn the walls of the great terraced temple at Der-el-Bahri?

I saw a cast of this bas-relief in the Metropolitan Museum of Art in New York. Like most Egyptian art, it was as crammed with explanatory text as a modern comic strip. It showed a formidable-looking black queen and her retinue; round domed huts with high-set doors reached by ladders; African animals and plants. In the next panels it showed, as if after a lapse of time, the imported goods beautifying Egypt: on every side ornaments of gold and ebony, boxes of perfumes and aromatic gums, elephant tusks, and ostrich plumes. Transplanted trees from Punt were pictured in bloom. This wasn't fantasy; in our time, archaeologists found dried roots of myrrh trees in the hot yellow sand at Der-el-Bahri.

Egypt had strenuous dealings, through many centuries, with a black people whom it called Nubians—its neighbors to the south, far down the Nile. Nubia could be reached, despite rough and dangerous waters around the cataracts. So the Egyptians infiltrated it as early as 2400 B.C. and ruled it intermittently. For a while a viceroy was in charge of the whole area, overseeing the building of towns and forts and temples.

Having been Egyptianized, the Nubians served in the Egyptian army and held government posts. Wooden models in tombs were replicas of Nubian archers (captives? mercenaries? volunteers?) in ranks beside Egyptian spearmen. A wall painting from the reign of Tutankhamen, 1361–52 B.C., depicted Nubian princes paying him homage; they brought him gold, leopard skins, and giraffe tails.

But then "African nationalism" became as inflammatory an issue in the Nile valley as it would be throughout Africa in our day. The Nubians rebelled again and again. They grew so strong and so skilled in guerrilla fighting that they forced their conquerors to grant them independence around 760 B.C. By then the Egyptians weren't particularly good soldiers, and in 751 B.C. the Nubians turned the tables completely, invading behind war elephants and putting their own kings on Pharaoh's throne.

After only seventy years the Assyrians "came down like a wolf on the fold" with new iron weapons and drove the Nubians out of Egypt. But the Nubians' own kingdom—which they called Cush—was just beginning centuries of grandeur.

Separated by seas of sand and rock from much of the world, no longer threatened by Egypt, the Nubians developed a remarkable civilization. They constructed a big ironworks in the desert. They sent overland expeditions as far west as Lake Chad. They built ports on the Red Sea, and traded with Arabia, East Africa, India, and maybe even China of the Han dynasty.

We learned of their trade because Nubian ostrich eggs went into Mycenaean tombs of 125 B.C.; Nubian ambassadors were in Rome in the first century B.C.; an official of the Nubian queen Candace was in a chariot on "the road that goeth down from Jerusalem to Gaza" sometime after the crucifixion when he encountered one of Christ's twelve disciples, Philip. The apostle "preached unto him" and finally baptized him. (Acts 8) As late as the fourth century A.D. a Greek writer named Heliodorus confected a romantic epic about a Nubian princess who supposedly married a Greek dignitary. (Greek men insisted on virgin brides, and the Nubians could offer guarantees. They practiced the cruel art of infibulation, which was the attachment of a ring or lock to the genitals to prevent copulation.)

The Nubian civilization finally fell prey to nomad invaders about 320 A.D. Then it was almost totally forgotten until 1772, when a traveler, James Bruce, sighted a few imposing ruins lying like noble hulks aground in the waste of the Butana desert. He wrote about them in a book, which most readers disbelieved. It did eventually arouse curiosity among archaeologists, however.

I was curious too.

I stopped in the Sudan to look at the bones of the greatest of inner Africa's civilizations. Under a merciless sun in the vast sandy void, seemingly alone in time as in space, were brick pyramids that had contained a list of seventy-two consecutive Nubian kings spanning a thousand years. Many miles farther were dry reservoirs, slag heaps from iron foundries, and worked-out gold mines sometimes a hundred feet deep.

At a place called Musawwarat I saw a complex of crumbling pillared temples once sheathed in sparkling white gypsum, where Nubians had bowed down before their many-armed lion god, which was strangely reminiscent of India's Siva. Nearby was a massive affair of walls and ramps—probably a stable for elephants. I saw elegant portraits of these animals decorating its stonework.

Remnants of the Nubians' lavish masonry towns dotted the desert elsewhere. But I felt no aura, no ghosts anywhere. To me, the Nubians were lifeless and inscrutable. No one had deciphered their writing. No one had done enough excavating to understand what sort of lives they led. We know only that their civilization was rich and powerful, and that it intermingled with Egypt and other great nations.

So I flew on. I was headed deeper south—to Rhodesia, where an even lesser-known black civilization had also traded with Egypt.

# 11

# Reach Into Darkness

Analyzing cosmetics used by an Egyptian princess, a chemistry professor found that some of them contained antimony, used for making a powder to darken eyelids. Antimony was not mined in Egypt, nor were the antimony mines of Persia and Turkey in operation until much later. If the Egyptians used antimony in the time of the sixth dynasty it could have come only from Rhodesia, the professor reasoned.

Such links between inner Africa and the dead civilizations I had photographed in Europe were in my mind through the long hours of my flight to Rhodesia.

The great cultures of antiquity apparently sent emissaries into the Dark Continent, but if they brought back information it died with their own cultures. I knew that a Cretan fresco from 1600 B.C. portrayed a Minoan officer leading black troops. A cave painting found in South Africa showed a man somersaulting over an onrushing animal, in the manner of the bull leaping portrayed by vase paintings and murals at Knossos. The Minoans' symbol of the double ax was on gold ear-pieces worn by Zulu, Swazi, and Tanzanian tribes—and on the dazzling vermilion *kente* cloth traditionally worn by the proud Ashanti people even in our time.

Did the Ashanti know Mycenae and Crete? They made pure gold masks for chiefs, like those Schliemann found at Agamemnon's citadel. One magnificent Ashanti mask was only seven inches high but weighed almost three and a half pounds. Their Golden Stool, displayed only on rare occasions of state, was once photographed laden with delicately wrought talismans: golden masks, images, handcuffs, bells.

Ashanti legend said that the stool floated down from the sky in a cloud of dust, amid thunder, sometime before our Middle Ages. That would have been much too late for Mycenae—but the Ashanti might be older than they realized. They believed that their history went back to the beginning of time, when their first ancestor crawled out of Lake Bosumtwi, a gloomy jungle mire that intermittently belched gas and mud.

Africa was known, somehow, in classical times. Carthage hired black mercenaries in the Punic Wars. Virgil's epic of the Trojan War mentioned "Africa, breeding ground of the great," and the naturalist Pliny marveled, "Always something new out of Africa."

Homer too heard of Africa. He referred to it as a fit place for gods' vacations. He sang of Odysseus landing in the land of the lotus eaters, "where it seemed always afternoon," which some investigators thought was Libya. Other classical heroes were definitely reported in "Libya." Thucydides mentioned a group from Troy who were swept there by a storm. When Diomedes returned to Tiryns and found a usurper in power, he went off to "Libya." These references misled me until I happened to stumble on a fact mentioned in few books: "Libya" was the Greek word for "Africa."

Perseus, the legendary founder of Tiryns, must

have been in Africa if, as tales said, he married a black princess. This would make their great-grandson Hercules an octoroon.

Our own civilization knew little of Africa's lost cultures until black researchers went to work about 1950. They gathered and translated old Arabic works. They went deep into the interior to find minnesingers, who, like Homer, remembered and recited the communal past in vast detail. One Rhodesian chief, according to Laurens Lloyd, blinded a bard to make sure he stayed in the village.

The Arabic reports were full of detail, and kept the Dark Continent a shimmering vision of hearsay for generations. I saved something written by the great Moorish geographer al-Bakri of Cordoba about 1070 A.D.

> The king of Ghana can put 200,000 warriors in the field, more than 40,000 armed with bow and arrow.
>
> When he gives audience . . . he sits in a pavilion around which stand horses caparisoned in cloth of gold; behind him stand pages holding gold-mounted swords; on his right hand are sons of the princes of his empire, splendidly clad, with gold plaited into their hair.

That Ghana vanished long ago, swallowed by invading Moroccans. Seven centuries later, in 1957, Ashanti advocates of a "new" Africa resurrected the ancient name and bestowed it on a former British colony, the Gold Coast, several hundred miles southeast of the original Ghana.

The truth of al-Bakri's writings was proved in part by statistics in his travel book, giving distances between Ghana's cities and markets. Checked in modern times, many of these proved accurate. Archaeologists dug up towns that al-Bakri had described, and found ruins of tall stone mansions.

Old Ghana probably was larger than modern France. It lay in the southeast corner of modern

Mauritania. Its great capital, Kumbi, with perhaps thirty thousand residents, was the terminus of a perilous caravan trail that led across the Sahara to Morocco, carrying gold nuggets from Ghana's streams. Nobles and chiefs collected taxes and customs duties, monopolizing on the king's behalf all gold found in the kingdom.

Astute middlemen in the gold commerce were founders of trading posts that grew to be great medieval states in the western Sudan. Ghana was the first of these. Native bards said it was already flourishing by the seventh century A.D.

What could caravans bring that was worth gold? Mostly salt, at first.

As in other places where this mineral didn't occur, salt was prized in the Sudan. Oasis dwellers in the Sahara dug it from the sand in thick slabs and sent it south on camels.

The gold-salt exchange made cities civilized as well as rich. One trade center, Awdoghast, was praised by al-Bakri as "a very large city with several markets, many date palms and henna trees . . . filled with fine houses and solid buildings."

In 1352 A.D. the best-traveled man of the Middle Ages, Ibn Batuta, joined a caravan across the Sahara, and sojourned a year in Mali. It was almost unknown, despite the fact that it was bigger and wealthier (at least in gold and salt) than Egypt. Mali had replaced Ghana as Africa's grandest imperial system. Ibn Batuta said that on audience days the sultan stalked from his palace "preceded by musicians who carry gold and silver musical instruments, and behind him come three hundred slaves."

The sultan wore a "velvety red tunic" and golden skullcap. He dispensed judgments from a silk-carpeted dais under "a sort of pavilion made of silk, surmounted by a bird fashioned in gold about the size of a falcon." An executioner stood ready nearby.

Ibn Batuta was more impressed by the court's justice than by its grandeur. "Of all peoples, the Negroes are those who most abhor injustice. Their sultan shows no mercy to one guilty. There is complete safety in their land. Neither traveler nor inhabitant has anything to fear from robbers or violence."

Ibn Batuta's stories, like Marco Polo's, were often greeted with reserve. But explorers eventually found that most of what he wrote was true. Mali dazzled cosmopolitan Arab visitors with its stone palace, ebony throne, and ranks of trumpeters and drummers.

Even in 1500, when Mali was in steep decline, another famous traveler confirmed Ibn Batuta's verdict on its attainments. Leo Africanus described the capital on the Niger River as a town of six thousand many-windowed homes and several schools. Its people, he said, were versatile craftsmen and brainy merchants, superior to "all other Negroes in wit, civility and industry." No doubt part of their industry was bred by the national custom of chaining the feet of schoolboys who were slow to memorize the Koran.

A Mali emperor literally put his empire on the world map when he made a pilgrimage to Mecca in 1324. His entourage included five hundred slaves, each with a four-pound gold bar. Everyone along his route profited as he passed. The gold he dumped into circulation caused inflation that lasted twelve years in Cairo. News spread slowly in those days, but as time passed the tale of Mali's wealth lured treasure seekers to Africa. One Egyptian, Sheik Uthman ed-Dukkali, sent back word that Mali was "four months of travel long and four months wide." In any case, no imperial realm except the Mongol Empire was geographically larger at that time.

For all its piety and industry, the Mali state eventually rotted like Imperial Rome. About 1360 it fell into a convulsion of regicides, usurpations, and palace revolutions that lasted thirty years. By then, three neighboring states had bitten off chunks of it. Yet Mali took another century to die.

By then western Africa's most powerful and urbane principality was Songhai, ruled by converted Muslims like earlier black states. After seizing the throne in a military coup, Askia Muhammad founded a university and gave Songhai a long-lasting tradition of intellectual vigor. The cultural capital was fabled old Timbuktu, captured from Mali, and as inaccessible to infidels as was Mecca. Leo, a Muslim, visited during Askia's reign and was received graciously by "numerous judges, doctors, and clerics, all paid well by their king. He accords great respect to men of learning."

Peripatetic Muslim scholars journeyed to Timbuktu to sharpen their minds. Islam had no strict orthodoxy, and welcomed ideas from the black sages. They lectured often and wrote prolifically. Their labors led Leo to observe that in Timbuktu the book and manuscript trade was more profitable than any other commerce.

But it wasn't books that kept Timbuktu's name in the mouths of traders. This great caravan city on the fringe of the Sahara was awash with gold. Leo wrote:

> Rich merchants travel constantly about the region with their wares. A great many Blacks bring quantities of gold, but never find enough goods on which to spend all their gold, and always take half or two-thirds home.

Outsiders never knew where the gold lodes were. Europe and Islam ached to find out, because the Old World's gold reserves were dwindling. In search of adventure as well as vast wealth, many a wanderer went out to try his luck in Africa. Most disappeared. But a few struck it rich.

One who didn't was a Catalan captain named Jacme Ferrer, who sailed in a galley from Majorca to find "the river of gold" in western Africa, and was never heard from again. One who did was a certain Anselm d'Isalguier, who came safely home with an African princess as his bride. She was attended by African servants, one of whom practiced medicine. His herbs and elixirs must have seemed potent, for he was called to treat the Dauphin Charles, heir to the French throne.

The great Florentine banking house of Portinari sent out a resourceful agent, Benedetto Dei, who actually got to Timbuktu and set up business arrangements with Songhai in the 1470s. His dealings were so secret that few reports survived for posterity.

Perhaps he closed doors behind him. For the next three centuries no other white traveler was known to survive in the African interior. But ships that anchored off the western coast came back heavy with gold from somewhere inland. England's Queen Elizabeth cleared a thousand-pound profit on one voyage.

What was happening to those great civilizations in the silent interior? Apparently their caravan routes lengthened and proliferated, bringing new kingdoms to birth and setting them against one another. Raids by neighbors cut off Songhai's camel trains and made glamorous Timbuktu a ghost town. When René Caillié, a French adventurer, reached Timbuktu in 1828 it was only a "mass of ill-looking houses of earth," except for a few crumbling edifices left from earlier centuries.

Meanwhile, a new confederation of tribes became the Ashanti, whose fierce sense of nationhood survives to this day. Ashanti country included about one third of present-day Ghana. That territory was the archetypal western Africa I'd read about in *Heart of Darkness:* silent streams in the gloom of great trees and tangled undergrowth, opening into villages of mud, thatch, and corrugated iron. I couldn't visualize a true civilization arising there.

But the Ashanti capital, Kumasi, startled white visitors. In 1817 an Englishman, T. Edward Bowdich, was met by bands of flutes, horns, and drums, and by companies of warriors bedecked with rams' horns, eagles' feathers, seashells, leopards' tails, bells, amulets, and quivers of poisoned arrows. He found the city scrupulously clean, with wide streets and pruned trees. Each house had a lavatory, flushed with boiling water. Rubbish was burned daily. The royal palace covered five acres, like Buckingham Palace.

When the residents of Kumasi were driven out by Sir Garnet Wolseley's troops in the six-week Ashanti War of 1873, its treasuries of gold artwork were auctioned off and shipped to England by the officers who bought it. Then they blew up the palace. Every other kingdom in western Africa received similar ministrations from European powers at about that time.

Not all Africa's gold was moving north across the Sahara or west to the Atlantic. Far to the east, other great commercial monarchies rose and thrived on the demand for gold—but not just for gold alone. Ivory, iron, tortoise shell, rhinoceros horn, palm oil—and slaves—were put aboard Indian and Arab dhows that plied the coasts of what are now Somalia, Kenya, and Tanzania.

Inexplicably, this east-coast trade, too, had begun in very ancient times. A sailors' guide written in Greek and published by some unknown scribe in the second or third century A.D. described coastal conditions in the Red Sea and Indian Ocean as far south as modern Tanzania.

Over the centuries this trade expanded, mostly by Arab doings—though at least two large Chinese fleets might have anchored their towering hulls off Africa's eastern shores. An African giraffe appeared in a Chinese painting from 1414.

The trade nurtured rich coastal emporiums—Kilwa, Malindi, Barawa, Mogadisho, Sofala, and others. Black merchants bought (for themselves and their land partners) Eastern fabrics, steel tools and daggers, beads, spices, and porcelain. The biggest and most cultivated city, to judge from ruins visible in our time, was Mogadisho, but the wealthiest and most important were Sofala and Kilwa.

Sofala's iron mines were legendary. So were its gold ingots, prized for their purity. Sofala built a twelve-story stone tower that awed all beholders. (Why, I wondered, did it want a tower? This question was to perplex me again, when I saw Zimbabwe.) The town became Portuguese in the sixteenth century, which ultimately finished it. By our time it was almost a ghost town. Its ruined fortifications were partly submerged in the ocean. (Oddly, the only Sanskrit word I encountered in Africa was "Sofala"—which means "beautiful shore.")

Kilwa, nine hundred miles north, was "one of the most beautiful and well-constructed towns in the world," wrote Ibn Batuta, the same globe trotting diarist who later visited Mali. It had a mint, the first in Africa. Its gardens were lush with fruit. Milton's *Paradise Lost* mentioned it by its Portuguese form, "Quiloa."

I wandered in its ruins, hemmed by dense underbrush. A silent cavern of stone columns and arches had been the first and biggest mosque in eastern Africa, built in the thirteenth century. The black sultan's clifftop palace was enormous, covering about two acres. I counted a hundred rooms plus galleries and patios. There had been elaborate washing arrangements and a fresh-water bathing pool.

The Kilwa merchants were indispensable men in a vast network. Their inland trading contacts reached Lake Nyasa, and might even have spread across the continent to the empire of Mali. On the backs of donkeys and camels, on the heads of porters, in the holds of barges and dhows, tons of goods went through Kilwa and the other coastal cities. Just as trans-Saharan trade wove Africa's western hinterlands into flamboyant empires, so the Indian Ocean coastal trade built civilizations on the plateau of mid-Africa. In the fullness of time they all died and disappeared.

Of numerous lost kingdoms on that vast steppe, the most mysterious thrived between the Zambezi and Limpopo rivers, ruled from a place now called Zimbabwe. This was my camera crew's prime target in Africa.

Zimbabwe was a famous enigma. It was old when Africa's medieval gold empires were young. Nevertheless, tribal legends ignored it, except for vague murmurs that some evil god had created it.

No paintings in Europe and no inscriptions in Egypt showed any knowledge of it. Nowhere in the world, apparently, was there any specific myth or folk tale or native memory that might relate to Zimbabwe. I wondered why natives in the vicinity insisted that they knew nothing of its history.

The first white known to have seen the site died there. He was a German named Adam Render, who left his family because of some scandal and went to Africa. In 1868, alone in the veld 292 miles south of Salisbury and 179 miles east of Bulawayo, he stumbled onto huge brush-choked ruins. What else he found there nobody knows. The place must have been attractive to him, for he returned several times.

In 1871 ivory hunters found his body there, too decomposed to give any clue. Inevitably, rumors spread that he was murdered for hidden treasure. A gold rush began. Soldiers, explorers, prospectors, reporters, gentlemen antiquaries, and other assorted characters made their way to the site—and dug enthusiastically, making no records of whatever artifacts they found.

They dug up soapstone carvings, a few gold bangles, and numerous objects perhaps used in sexual or fertility rites. But no treasure. The site was abandoned to archaeologists, who began an erudite uproar that raged for years.

At first, whites refused to believe that Zimbabwe's massive battlements and towers could have been built by blacks. No natives were ever skilled enough, they maintained. They theorized, variously, that the ruins were of Phoenician origin and might be the Ophir of the Bible; were built by Nubians or Egyptians, and might be the lost land of Punt; were the work of wandering Arabs; were old Roman ruins; and so on. Among those excited by such theories was H. Rider Haggard, who used them as ingredients for *King Solomon's Mines,* a hugely popular African adventure novel still found today in public libraries.

Until almost the end of the nineteenth century, no white man had seen anything like Zimbabwe. But when the great British imperialist Cecil Rhodes opened the region to settlement, immigrants discovered hundreds of similar (but smaller) stone structures scattered in the lonely veld of the central southern plateau—not only in Rhodesia but in Mozambique and Bechuanaland too.

This aroused a new generation of scholars. Some thought the buildings showed the architectural style of Etruscan stoneworks in Sardinia—which meant Egypt had transmitted Etruscan influence into Africa, they said. Others pointed out that surprisingly similar conical towers of rock were to be seen in Peru, the Balearics, the Shetland and the Orkney islands, the

Hebrides, and the north of Scotland—for which they could offer no explanation.

Mapping the discoveries, they saw that Zimbabwe was the center of approximately 350,000 square miles speckled with stone defense works, mostly the conical towers. Groping for a culture that might have designed this elaborate pattern of defense, students of African lore ascertained that around 1440 A.D. there had been a far-flung system ruled by a monarch whose hereditary title, Monomotapa, gave the domain its name.

He made Zimbabwe the storage place for gold and other treasure to be sent out to the coast—or so the Portuguese of his time believed, when they negotiated with him in attempts to locate "the gold of Ophir." Their writings mentioned "a fortress built of large and heavy stones . . . in the middle of this country." In 1518 a Portuguese agent, Duarte Barbosa, reported that the Monomotapa ruler was "a great lord with many kings under him."

Later this empire was ruled by another dynasty of lords, the Rozwi. They were skilled builders. I saw some of their empty stone villages, now overgrown by brush, between the Zambezi River and the Orange Free State.

In 1950 an odd fact emerged. Although the Monomotapa and later the Rozwi had indeed used Zimbabwe as the assembly point for trains of porters who slogged through the thick forests to Safala and other market towns on the coast, they hadn't built Zimbabwe. It was there before them.

This was established by carbon-14 tests of organic matter from the ruins. The site had been occupied or at least visited by human beings ever since the Stone Age. Some of the granite walls apparently were built between 400 and 700 A.D., in Europe's Dark Ages. Others seemed to have been added in the thirteenth century.

Why this interval of a half millennium? Zimbabwe remained unexplained. But there was one near-certainty: it almost had to have been the work of natives.

Who were the natives of central Africa between,

say, 1000 B.C. and 1000 A.D.? Shreds of surviving evidence indicated that they were cattle herders who sometimes lived in villages of unknown size. They knew how to make iron spears and farming tools as early as 500 B.C.

These pioneers were called Bantu, a word that simply meant "the people." They lived first in forests near the coast. At some time in prehistory they began to swarm into the central plateau—perhaps to put space between themselves and other people who kept arriving from the Sahara as it dried into a desert after 2500 B.C.

The Bantu migration was a slow drift and scatter. People packed and went farther on when they felt they had too many neighbors, or when a place got quarrelsome, or when they feared magic around them. This moving-on process covered almost two thousand years, during which about four hundred Bantu dialects arose—all closely related, like the Romance languages. Just as the many little principalities that spoke Romance languages inherited features of Rome's civilization, changing it by their own folkways and later experiences, so the tribes that spoke Bantu diversified their common inheritance. As they migrated they often met non-Bantu peoples (pygmies and Hottentots, for example) with whom they traded and sometimes interbred.

Bantu oral tradition said nothing about building.

"No archaeological sites traceable to them have yet been found," said Dr. Jan Vansina of the University of Wisconsin, probably the world's chief authority on early peoples of the African interior. Nevertheless, Bantu dialects were the only ones native to the Zimbabwe area for as far back as experts could probe. Therefore, the builders of Zimbabwe must have been either a Bantu kingdom or some non-Bantu civilization that left nothing to posterity.

By common consent the place was given a Bantu name meaning "royal court," or "great place" or "venerated houses" or "stone houses" or "great house," depending on the dialect. The white who named it was Frederick Selous, a celebrated hunter, explorer, and collector of museum specimens, who wandered through the country shooting elephants long before Rhodes cast his eye on it. When he christened the site "Zimbabwe" nobody ventured alternate suggestions. Today, Rhodesia's black leaders want to assert their nation's black heritage by renaming it Zimbabwe. (Already one of the best hotels in Rhodesia is called the Hotel Monomotapa.)

I drove to Zimbabwe, which took a day.

First, endless veld baked under yellow sun. The road was poor and I jounced along for hours, inhaling the hot straw smell of brown grass, the rusty smell of unseen animals, the dust like red paprika in the hot air.

Then parkland—dotted here and there, as far as my eye could see, with just one kind of round dark-green shrub and one kind of tree, the African acacia, with branches like spokes of an umbrella, spreading into a flat top beautifully adapted to catch maximum moisture during the scanty rains. The grass was gray-green.

At last in the far distance along the heat-blurred horizon I saw upthrust black shapes: granite hillocks. The country was rising a little. There were groves of trees, and some were gaudy trees that the Boers named kaffir boom, as big as oaks and covered with red blossoms.

I remembered someone saying that Zimbabwe gets more rain than the endless bush country around it. I imagine this meant more to its occupants than gold.

I sighted the first of the ruins atop the highest granite-shouldered promontory on the horizon. As I approached, the place seemed graceful rather than grim—for the big walls were tapered and curved instead of straight, and their entrances bent invitingly inward, so there were no sharp angles. Their top rows of granite slabs slanted vertically to form a pattern of airy chevrons.

At the foot of the majestic walls, I was momentarily hypnotized by their beauty. A bright pink vine overgrew them in places. Sandalwood and fig trees threw odd inky shadows. The varying blue-gray granite blocks fit trimly together without mortar, and were laid in smooth horizontal rows. How had so many thousands of rock pieces been cut into nearly uniform rectangles?

The ruins spread from the hilltop six hundred yards south, all enclosed by the great oval outer wall. After fifteen-odd centuries the wall still seemed immensely strong. It was seventeen feet thick at the base and twenty to thirty feet high. Along the top, monoliths pointed to the sky like fingers. They were decorative, but I wondered if heads had been impaled on them in bygone eras.

Looking down across the great enclosure, I tried to see the pattern of its internal layout. At first there seemed no plan. Amid the rubble I could make out foundations of near-circles, circles, platforms, intersecting walls, and long winding alleys, all open to the sky. At the far end was a massive stone ellipse a hundred yards long, surrounding other ruins within. It was known as the Temple. A squat-looking tower stood within it. There were marks of an efficient drainage system.

The convolutions put me in mind of the Knossos labyrinth. But then I realized that the builders had set these granite walls into the pattern of Africa's own circular mud-and-thatch villages. But there was an exception: the heavy intricate stoneworks known as the Acropolis, crowning the ninety-foot bluff.

I felt the late afternoon sun on my neck like a hot paw, but I was determined to prowl the ruins. First the Acropolis. It was a series of roofless stone rooms, one leading into another without visible resemblance to an African village or to any other plan. Again, I finally made sense of the arrangement. The rooms were lined up so that the rock outcrops and boulders served for walls wherever possible. Then the builders burrowed in behind rocks to create caves. This giant worms' nest, so to speak, could have been easily defended.

There were eerie acoustics in a cave below the walls of the Acropolis, as a guide demonstrated to me. Speaking in the cave, he could be heard clearly in the

Temple, a quarter mile away, but nowhere else in Zimbabwe. Witch doctors presumably made terrifying use of this phenomenon.

I clambered through broken walls and down winding steps to the spectacular Temple, which probably wasn't exactly a temple. African jungle civilizations built no temples, so far as we know. Their shrines were huts hidden in the bush.

The Temple at Zimbabwe was where the king dwelled with his wives, courtiers, and servants. There had been granaries, huts, and platforms inside the ellipse—which meant that this grandiose stone version of a tribal chief's compound was probably used for daily chores as well as for ceremonial rites, all hidden.

The Temple wall was fifteen feet thick and contained fifteen thousand tons of cut stone, experts estimated. Why such a formidable redoubt when the huge outer wall already encircled the whole Zimbabwe complex? Did the kings fear their own tribesmen? Or did they plan to hold out even if invaders penetrated the first stone oval?

Just inside the Temple wall, dominating the enclosure, was the conical windowless tower, probably Africa's most mysterious single structure. It was mysterious because it was solid masonry. There was no way to get to the top from inside—nor from outside, unless one used rope or ladder. What was the purpose of this tower?

It was surprisingly thick—fifty-eight feet at its base. It was only thirty feet high, although it had been five feet higher until one early gold hunter managed to scale the exterior granite facing and pried off five feet of blocks before he satisfied himself that there was no crypt inside. Confirming this judgment, another tower only half as high stood nearby. Its top half had been pushed over by a tree that had grown beside it. I could see that both halves were stonework to the core.

I had a wild thought. Could a few Africans fly a little, or levitate?

Someone with self-made wings like those of the

legendary Icarus might need the tower as a launching device for gliding, swooping flights. Winged men might also flap to the top of Zimbabwe's broad walls, which might explain why there were no ramps or stairways. I thought again of Sofala's seemingly useless twelve-story tower.

A supernatural ability to soar was often mentioned in Hindu scriptures, and supposedly was an attribute of certain Catholic saints. Joseph of Cupertino (1603–66) rose inadvertently so often, according to church records, that his superiors forbade him to attend choir.

Well, airborne men were as good an explanation as any other I could think of for the strange towers. I turned away. The sun was low, and the whole place began to seem unpleasant.

I imagined the blacks who had first lived here and departed mysteriously. I sensed something sleek and feminine about them—something sly and—yes—sinister. This was the meaning, to me, of the roundness of every thick wall at ends and openings, the subtle curves of passageways, the slanted-W patterns that ran around the tops of the walls. There was abnormal refinement in the smallness of the blocks into which the granite was cut, and in the very softness of their color.

Zimbabwe's builders were unlike the hearty Nubian miners, the trumpet-playing gold tycoons of Ghana and Mali and the Congo, the prancing Ashanti warriors. They worshiped different gods in silent little courts of the Temple and around the squat tower. They would have been soft-voiced, delicate in their gestures, horribly refined even in dealing with their victims.

Lingering alone among the ruins at sunset put unpleasant fancies in my mind. Shadows were creeping near. The silence was ominous. When my footsteps broke it, echoes along the stone passages lasted too long.

As I left that haunted citadel, and imagined the huge labors that had gone into building it, I felt the ruthlessness of the rulers as all the more sinister for their femininity. Were they Bantu people in some upsurge of knowledge that passed away? Or were they a nonesuch, lost forever in limbo? Probably we will never know.

Months later I learned that Zimbabwe also had an unpleasant effect on the noted South African historical novelist Stuart Cloete, although he got a somewhat different feeling than I. He wrote:

> I had a feeling of things having happened here when I stood under the walls of Zimbabwe—of blood and cruelty, of strange rites and sacrifices, of lust. This was a haunted place, though not by ghosts that I could feel. Not that I believe in ghosts.

I went from the dead to the living. I went to find the remarkable Dogon tribe.

# 12

# Africa's Tribe of Mystics

The Dogons believed they had descended from a star that had zigzagged toward the earth. The star was the one we call Sirius, brightest in the sky. At least these were the reports. They intrigued me for several reasons.

One: I'd never heard of any other black tribe or kingdom identifying specific stars or even showing much interest in them. Africa's interior civilizations apparently kept no calendars.

Two: Sirius—known as the Dog Star because it is the most noticeable member of the constellation Canis Major—was uniquely interesting to the ancient Egyptians, who called this star Sept. They seemed to be less advanced astronomically than their Sumerian contemporaries, but they knew enough to predict approximately the day on which the Nile would rise. This was the day each year when Sirius appeared just before sunrise. Egypt dated each calendar year from this annual "rising of Sept" in mid-July, promptly followed by the Nile floods, which watered and fertilized their fields.

Three: Sirius did indeed wobble slightly from year to year.

I wanted to know how the Dogons had picked Sirius as their ancestor—and had noticed, or been told, that it zigzagged.

They were in the Republic of Mali, which contained all that was left of Timbuktu, Africa's most learned ancient city. For me this meant another long trek inland from the great bend of the Niger River—again crossing grasslands tawny as a lion's mane, without a tree in sight all day. Stopping at villages, I sometimes saw Dogon woodcarvings, grotesque and oddly proportioned figurines.

There were no Dogons in these villages, but just their carvings were worth study. African tribal sculpture was seldom made to be enjoyed as "art." Carvings had religious functions. Each was meant to attract and house a specific ghost—perhaps an ancestor or dead chief. Unless a ghost was happy within a carving, the Dogons thought, it might roam in anger and harm a village. (Remember the Etruscan belief?)

Unused by a spirit, a carving had no value to Dogons. When it began to rot or was gnawed by white ants, it was considered unsuitable as a home, so another figure was whittled to replace it. The first piece, no matter how artistic, was set aside as worthless, whereupon a non-Dogon might buy it.

In all Dogon figures I saw, the head was disproportionately large. I knew this had been done deliberately; the carvings were too skilled technically to be proportioned by chance. Believing the head to be where the spirit was, Dogon sculptors gave it about one third or one quarter of the body. Unlike classical Greeks and Etruscans, who thought the liver was the seat of life, a Dogon sculptor sensed that the skull was paramount. He wanted to express the spiritual nature of reality by portraying people as they *were,* not as they looked.

At last I found a Dogon village, sheltered in a grim sandstone escarpment. The buildings were like no other structures I had ever seen. Formed of clay, they looked like huge pieces of pottery, except that their bases merged with the reddish-brown desert ground. It was as if the buildings bulged up out of the ground instead of being built.

As I looked at the people I knew they weren't Bantu. They were wiry, instead of heavily muscled. Their heads were round, with kinky hair. They had broad flat noses and thick lips. Their skins ranged from dark brown to blue-black. These characteristics put them in the west African or "true" Negro category rather than Bantu, who were generally lighter and shorter, with facial features closer to the European mold.

They were friendly but spoke no English. Some spoke French—Mali used to be the French Sudan—but my French wasn't attuned to theirs.

The French ethnologist Marcel Griaule wrote that after living with the Dogons of the western Sudan he had abandoned "all previous ideas about the mentality of black peoples." Griaule told how he had listened to an old blind man named Ogotommeli for more than a month, and how this sage laid out an intricate mythology of man and the universe that displayed "an internal coherence, a secret wisdom, and an apprehension of realities equal to that which we Europeans conceive ourselves to have attained."

My trek carried me from village to village. The typical Dogon village was built on steep slopes in the crevices of cliffs—a tangle of clay huts among granaries and outbuildings, all surrounded by walls, giving an air of proud, inaccessible majesty that reminded me of old Tuscan cities.

The Dogons apparently settled in the Bandiagara cliffs between the tenth and thirteenth centuries, in flight from Muslim invaders. According to their oral history they came from the ancient Mande kingdom, in what is now western Mali. The hundred miles of cliffs parallel to the Niger gave safety from slave-seeking horsemen.

So as not to waste arable land, they built their villages on the rock. But their material wants were few and simple. They eked out what others might call a subsistence living, with no visible sadness or acquisitiveness. They lived in peace until the French arrived in 1893 and "pacified" the area. No census has ever been taken, but approximately a quarter of a million Dogons are estimated to be clustered in the Bandiagara cliffs.

My talks with them were tantalizing. Whites in the vicinity were sometimes helpful until they realized I came from America, and were cool thereafter. Mali was leaning toward the communist view of the world.

I did learn that Dogons believed, like Western man, in a single, faraway, nonphysical god. He had made the earth by flinging a lump of clay from heaven, they said. Soon after this creation he put twins called Nummo on earth. They moved freely between sky and earth, bringing back celestial materials from which the first clothing was made.

This was all I got. I learned later that Griaule made his first field trip to Dogon country in 1931, and made annual visits until 1946 before the people trusted him enough to initiate him into what they called "deep knowledge." So perhaps I was lucky to learn as much as I did.

But I left Africa disappointed. Probably I would never know the Dogon story of how they had come to earth from Sirius, or how they perceived Sirius as weaving its way toward them. I was left with the mystery that a so-called primitive tribe had discovered a star invisible to the naked eye, and constructed their religion around the probability that the star was their original home. The incredible fact was that their legend held information which earthbound technology confirmed long after the tale was promulgated.

# 13

# The City Under the River

I disliked the man's face. Ugly? He was almost inhuman.

He watched me steadily through eyes narrowed to slits. Under heavy lids, the corners of his eyes seemed to squint at everyone and everything, vigilant for any deviation from his law. Impersonal but intent as a coiled cobra, he was clearly ready to lash out in any direction.

He might have been thirty years old or fifty. It was hard to guess. His face was hard, scarred, but unwrinkled. Probably few people gazed long enough at it to estimate its age; his heavy downturned lips discouraged conversation or even salutation. Just by being around, he would make people uneasy. From their first glance at his low brow and prognathous jaw, they would know that he wasn't very bright and wasn't ever merciful.

But he was bright enough to know that he was boss. The way he tilted his chin, thrusting it out from his bull-like neck, looking coldly down his ruined nose at me, was a mannerism of scornful authoritarians who applied inflexible rules and brooked no question. He was an ageless prototype of the Enforcer.

Even across forty centuries I could feel his livid conviction that anything opposing the law must be instantly smashed and flung out into the darkness beyond the walls. I didn't know his name or title but I thought I knew his post. He would have fidgeted on a parapet of the citadel, glaring down at the eighteen work platforms of the huge state granary in the heart of the ancient city of Mohenjo-Daro.

Perhaps you yourself have met his arrogant stare, and looked away. Did you ever skim through any illustrated books that mentioned the empire of which he was part, sometimes called the Indus Valley civilization, sometimes the Harappan culture? Most books on this subject show a picture of him. His head is one of a very few significant pieces of sculpture found in the buried city. More than that, it seems to personify a spirit of autocratic planning, which was implicit in that civilization. I saw the bust itself in the National Museum of Pakistan, and it sent a chill down my back.

I'm sure he wasn't a ruler. No tombs of a ruling class ever were found in the vast extent of the Indus Valley empire, so perhaps this peculiar people had no nobles in our sense of the term. In any case, the man had such a low forehead (not at all typical of skulls found there, incidentally) that he could hardly have been a planner or leader; he was pure fanatical monitor. This might make him a priest if the unknown religion was harsh enough.

Harappan civilization was a foursquare utilitarian business in some ways but mysterious in others, and it intrigued me. It played out a hidden drama in a seemingly empty desert. The first mystery was its origin.

The great scholar Sir Mortimer Wheeler (president of the Society of Antiquaries) said, "The Indus civilization appears to spring into being full grown." Unlike most cities, Mohenjo-Daro didn't evolve from a cowpath and huddle of huts. It was built from a chart, like our generation's Brasília or Century City or Islamabad, but without their scope for individuality.

The streets formed monotonous rectangular blocks. The brick walls were blank, with no paintings or carvings or ornamentation. However, the two-story homes were roomy and (I would guess) comfortable, with inside courtyards and toilets. Spacious public baths were like those of Imperial Rome two thousand years later. For water supply and wastes, the network of canals and pipes and sewers and inspection peepholes was described by experts as "the most complete and ingenious ever devised in antiquity."

Another mystery was its location.

The Indus basin is an oblong valley eight hundred miles long, one or two hundred across—an especially uninviting part of what today is India. Here and there it is stingily watered by the five rivers of the Punjab—Jhelum, Chenab, Ravi, Beas, and Sutlej—but tribes never lived in the basin. They preferred the uplands, which stood like a frame around the Indian scene, from Afghanistan at one end to Bhutan at the other, with the great Indus River tumbling out to water half a continent.

The Indus flows fast at first, as it begins its eighteen-hundred-mile descent to the Arabian Sea, and doubtless it nourished many primitive Punjab tribes at its cold and foaming source. But when it enters the gloomy wasteland of the Sind Desert near sea level, it declines in altitude only one foot per mile, and meanders majestically, sometimes switching course when the sands shift.

Into this forbidding but potentially fertile basin came the founders of the Indus Valley civilization. Venturing down from mountain villages in Iran or Afghanistan, they found the land leveling out. Perhaps for the first time in their lives, they saw flat horizon in all directions. And they discovered the Indian sun.

Temperatures reached 120 degrees F. Rainfall was so sparse than when it showered—so the natives say in our own day—one horn of a buffalo got wet, but not the other. The newcomers soon shed their shaggy garments of animal skins and their warm leg-wrappings. They improvised a cotton cloth swathed at the waist—augmented by warm shawls in the short winter, when the temperature dropped to the freezing point and the winds were biting.

The Sind was a cul-de-sac. The wanderers had either to climb the steep mountains they had descended or stay where they were. The only other place to go was the riverless Thar Desert on their left. But these people evidently knew something of farming, and were to make the broad basin of the Indus immensely productive.

We'll never know who led the expeditions onto the scorching plain, however hesitantly, and why others followed. But they must have been bold people with creative minds—pioneers in the full sense. At least they weren't exiles or drop-outs from the highlands. Maybe they were elite visionaries in search of El Dorado. Somewhere they had gotten the idea of a city, although they could scarcely have seen one, and couldn't hope to build one in the steep little valleys of their origin. They planned their city in detail before they built it, and planned organizational machinery that would make it work smoothly if somewhat grimly.

Some of them probably led forlorn lives and perished. Here and there on the Indus plain archaeologists found debris of villages older than Mohenjo-Daro. We might guess that attempts to colonize the valley went on intermittently, failure after failure, until one day a group won through.

Once settled on the flat banks of the Indus, their lives still wouldn't be serene. The annual snow-melt flood, swelling the river, would cover much of the landscape. This would renew the soil and, if contained, nourish rich crops. But the massive river could be terrible when it rose; it carried twice as much water as the Nile and ten times as much as the Colorado. So the struggle between farmers and floods never ended. An abnormal flood won sometimes, engulfing farms or even whole villages; three times or more, Mohenjo-Daro itself was almost washed away. Excavators of the city found thick layers of collapsed building material mixed with deep-packed silt from the muddy river. Among these were compensating platforms at different levels where inhabitants had rebuilt.

The menace of the river sparked "a story of human enterprise and understanding such as has occurred only a few times in the history and prehistory of mankind," as Sir Mortimer Wheeler said. The Indus Valley group eventually harnessed a great river system to the needs of its own vision. It reclaimed, cleared, embanked, and built canals across some 150,000 square miles of fruitful but endangered land.

Its land area became vaster than Egypt or Sumer —in fact, the vastest of any civilization before the Roman Empire. It covered a triangle with thousand-mile sides. The blunt apex of the triangle lay somewhere in the base of the Simla Hills (the foothills of the Himalayas) far up the Indus and its tributaries, perhaps as far as the Ganges. Its base spread eight hundred miles along the Arabian Sea, from about the modern Iran-Pakistan border to the Gulf of Cambay, a broad inlet just above today's Bombay.

Within this triangle were at least seventy towns. All used the same kinds of kitchenware, household tools, personal ornaments, and toys. Of course they had the same written language, which later would defy us. The whole expanse was flat. These people were lowlanders to the core, as befitted civilized folk.

Their gigantic triangle enclosed two cities, virtual twins: Mohenjo-Daro, about 400 miles inland, and Harappa, another 350 miles northeast on what then must have been a bank of the Ravi River, so the pair were linked by a continuous river thoroughfare.

Each city was three miles in circumference. Each had a population of about twenty thousand. Each was built of red mud bricks, with almost identical layout and architecture. But Harappa might easily have been built a generation or two later, as a sort of alternate capital, after Mohenjo-Daro went through its first serious flooding. The worst floods probably struck only at intervals of a century or two, and Harappa was safer because its river was smaller and meeker.

In fact, Himalayan snow and Punjab monsoon might have been only contributory factors in the floods that were sometimes so dangerous to Mohenjo-Daro. The prime factor might have been some tilting of land between city and coast. An earthquake spasm, or just a slow bulge during decades, could raise the shallow riverbottom a few inches—which might cause the meandering Indus to back up into ponds or lakes here and there. The results could be drastic. Flooding might be prolonged for years.

There were geologic deposits left by a hundred-mile lake not far below the city. Maybe this lake advanced up the valley toward Mohenjo-Daro, spreading slowly but relentlessly. The city might become an urban archipelago on heightened foundations in an inland sea.

Later (who could say how much later?) the earth might move again, or the Indus might eat its way through the natural dams, and the river could resume its normal path. Tons of debris and silt would be left. The city people would be forced to start their reclamation work anew.

But apparently natural forces were the only external threats. Neither Mohenjo-Daro nor Harappa was fortified except for its central citadel, roughly a quarter mile long and half as wide. Its mighty baked-brick wall, fifteen yards thick, was studded with bastions, ramps, and gates protected by guardrooms. But the military structure frowned inward, not outward. Sir Mortimer Wheeler dryly observed, "Its function may have been as much the affirmation of domestic authority as a safeguard against external aggression."

We could surmise how strong the domestic authority was from the fact that few weapons were found. The city's police seemingly felt safe in their citadel, and confident of their ability to control the populace without force of arms.

Probably they needed to control only the food supply. Unlike city people in Sumer and Egypt, the residents of Harappa and Mohenjo-Daro didn't leave their cities to work in the fields. Both cities were surrounded by clusters of farm towns, which evidently nourished them.

Huge quantities of grain must have funneled into the cities. The pattern of each city pointed to the huge granary as the economic focus of the civilization—its equivalent of our Federal Reserve Bank.

There was an unloading area where dusty, sweating drivers with their ox carts would have dumped the harvest from the fields. Above it was a platform onto which the sheaves of barley could be hauled by ropes. From there they could be stacked inside the citadel, and kept under guard until time for threshing.

The big circular brick work platforms each had a central hole in which stood a heavy wooden mortar. There was no doubt that these were threshing floors, and there was nothing surprising about their presence; much the same system of pounding grain with pestles still survives in Kashmir. What surprised me was that watchers from the citadel evidently kept the rows of workmen under stern scrutiny. Next to the platforms were a double row of barrackslike dwellings and a further range of immense granaries. The layout looked about as friendly as a penitentiary. The Indus Valley planners had some of the same thoughts as the totalitarians of our own century.

I walked through the silent city. The afternoon sun pressed its red light down the straight channels of the streets, making the buildings look like blocks of strawberry ice cream, but the total effect wasn't pleasant. Except for the color, this might have been the ruins of a 1926 factory town on the New Jersey flats or the Yorkshire moors, or of one of today's industrial cities in China or Russia.

Hundreds of roofless red-brick buildings, row after row and block after block, were identical. Their blank, windowless outer walls fronted on straight but narrow streets in which I could imagine the docile workers plodding toward the granary each morning. There were no big statues, no temples, no palaces, no theaters, no large open spaces that might have been athletic fields or even parade grounds. I wondered if the twenty thousand people who had lived there did much except work.

Still, the city wasn't altogether joyless. The main thoroughfares outside the center of the city were thirty feet wide, almost like modern boulevards. I saw a few shops. One contained sockets in the floor, possibly for wine jars, so it might have been a tavern. The bigger homes had private wells. Among the smaller ones were public wells where people must have gathered and gossiped. The city plan, as Sir Mortimer Wheeler saw it, was evidence of "middle-class prosperity with zealous municipal supervision."

I wondered about that "municipal supervision" and so did he. It was the big question mark of the Indus civilization. In a 1955 lecture, this eminent authority summed up his uncertainty after a quarter-century's study of the ruins:

> The citadel suggests that the folk-leaders who built it . . . had already been familiar with command and prestige. Our picture is that of a people led by rulers who may have had priestly attributes but, as their well-ordered towns and dwelling-houses prove, were essentially secular in outlook; sufficiently benevolent at any rate to nurture an uncommonly high general standard of living. . . .
>
> If we are right in assuming an early emergence of strong, focused rule accentuated by the rigorous conditions of the Indus valley, and in suspecting a correspondingly early and sudden emergence of the metropolitan citadel and the planned town—the oldest example, in fact, of the planned town known to us—we are confronted with a society which knew almost from the outset where it was going and what it was about.
>
> Unlike the civilizations of Mesopotamia and Egypt, it sprang into being fully organized, led by an intelligentsia which knew its own mind. Indeed so strong is the sense of a calculating personality and so sudden and complete its expression that I sometimes find myself wondering whether behind it all does not literally stand some powerful single mind, some great First Citizen.

After this hypothetical First Citizen went to his ancestors, the civilization endured for many centuries. What kept it going?

There were answers in the ruins. No civilization could live very long on the same acreage without putting down a layer of lost, broken, or discarded objects typical of their own period. After Harappa was unearthed by accident in 1921, and Mohenjo-Daro in 1924, archaeological expeditions spent every year up to the present systematically digging up stratified layers. Until those cities were discovered, historians supposed that India had been a seething tangle of primitive tribes before the taller, blond "Indo-Aryan" people migrated from the shores of the Caspian and introduced arts and sciences.

This was an error. The ruins of the two cities suggested that the great Indian juggernaut had picked up its cultural momentum before the beginning of its written history, which had started with the Indo-Aryans. The people of Mohenjo-Daro wove the same homespun cotton *khadi* as Gandhi. They wore the same gold and silver earrings, bangles, and nose studs as the village people of today. They used the same stone, copper, and bronze tools. They made charming little terracotta toys much like those of today—including two-wheeled carts, which are among our oldest examples of wheeled vehicles. They revered some of the same mother-goddesses and phallic images. They threw away quantities of the same sort of disposable clay cups, presumably because the Hindu taboo against drinking twice from the same cup had already been promulgated.

Yes, this ambiguous society had its creative aspects. Some of its jewelry was "so well finished and so highly polished," said Sir John Marshall, discoverer of Mohenjo-Daro, "that it might have come out of a Bond Street jeweler's rather than a prehistoric house of five thousand years ago."

Strangely, the lowest strata of these remains showed a more developed art than the upper layers—as if even the most ancient deposits were from an unknown society already hundreds, perhaps thousands, of years old. There was a provocative bronze figure of a dancing girl caught in mid-wriggle with hand on hip. And there were two extraordinary stone statuettes of male nudes. "When I first saw them I found it difficult to believe that they were prehistoric," Sir John Marshall reported. "Modelling such as this was unknown in the ancient world up to the Hellenistic age of Greece. The Greeks delighted in anatomical truth and took infinite pains to express it convincingly. In these two statuettes it is just this anatomical truth that is so startling, that makes us wonder whether Greek artistry could have been anticipated by sculptors of a far-off age."

However, as we might expect in such a practical business society, the richest store of artifacts was apparently for use in commerce. This treasure trove consisted of soapstone seals, usually about as big as postage stamps, probably used for marking bales of cotton or bags of grain. More than a thousand such seals turned up in Mohenjo-Daro. Others were found in cities of Mesopotamia and in the Persian Gulf, clues to the far-flung trade of this empire.

The seals delighted aesthetes and puzzled archaeologists. They were a delight because they were exquisitely carved with figures of bulls, elephants, antelope, and other animals. The artwork was so fine that it might have been done under a magnifying glass. A bas-relief of a bull was as vigorously delineated as a Renaissance cameo.

Archaeologists were puzzled for several reasons. The designs showed animals and scenes foreign to the Indus basin—a man up a tree with a tiger lurking hungrily below, for example. Such anomalies might mean that part of this treeless desert was jungle when the city was built.

The delicate pictographic inscriptions were another puzzle, and were studied intently because they were the chief surviving examples of Indus writing. About 250 different pictographs were identified—all as different from contemporary Egyptian hieroglyphics and Mesopotamian cuneiform as these two are from each other. But the longest single inscription contained just seventeen symbols. Tantalized, the philologists had to admit that civil servants were checking waybills and cargoes in the riverfront offices of Mohenjo-Daro and the magnificently equipped seaport on the Gulf of Cambay when the pyramids were a few hundred years old and Stonehenge was not yet built; here were details of their work, untranslatable.

A third puzzle of the seals was that occasionally they showed a bull-man, like Crete's Minotaur. Some Sumerian art, too, portrayed a Minotaur. Was there a hidden link between these civilizations and that of Knossos?

The seals were part of another, bigger mystery: the disappearance of civilization in the Indus basin. Toward the end of Mohenjo-Daro's long life, the quality of the seals fell off sadly. The soapstone was replaced by common clay, and crude geometric shapes replaced the lifelike engravings.

There were other symptoms of decline. Plain clumsy pots supplanted the earlier vivid and highly glazed ceramics. The city's systematic plan was abandoned. Around the great brick podium of the granary rose debris, interlaid with small untidy buildings. Fine well-made homes were partitioned into warrens for an obviously growing population. Streets were encroached on by shabby structures, or were choked by kilns that in better times would have been barred from residential zones.

New generations built on the collapsed foundations of their forebears, turning once-dignified neighborhoods into slums. The buildings at the topmost stratum were mere hovels.

But this didn't happen at Harappa, which gave no sign of slow degeneration. Apparently the life of that city stopped when it was at the height of prosperity. My guess was that its residents fled when they realized that their twin city was dying or dead. Some of them must have made their way to the hills, to be absorbed into villages that would pass along the cultural heritage perpetuated as India's. It would have been easier and quieter than Mohenjo-Daro's end.

I let my imagination crackle as I stood amid the

empty red-brown streets of Mohenjo-Daro. After a while I saw visions of the end.

It had been a day when dust storms swept the old city, I thought. Out beyond, enemies were massing, but no one in the citadel saw them. Whenever the fitful puffs of wind died, a brown-purple dust curtain hid the horizon. The sight close at hand was ugly enough: brown foamless edges of smooth and glassy rollers from the river, eating away the road.

The Indus had overflowed—days before, probably. So the crops were drowned, as in many recent years. Downriver, the desert had moved, so the course to the sea was choked with sand, and a mile-wide river was roaring.

There was fear in the city. The houses were above the flood—builders had seen to that after the last catastrophe—but the granaries were almost empty. No trading vessels had come down the Indus for a long time. Farm towns were deserted for miles around. The city had been emptying for days, though its people were merely scattering in panic. Nobody had made any plans.

The last of the faraway trees had been dragged in, years ago, and consumed in fires that baked the bricks. Now there could be no more bricks. Every vestige of vegetation on the ground had been cropped away by the people's goats and pigs and dogs, and by roving jackals. So there was nothing left to keep down the dust or slow the lake's spread, and little hope of scratching a living from the soil. The city was doomed at last.

In the heat and gloom the earth seemed to be dying of apoplexy. The dark ribbon of the steadily widening river wound through the dim landscape, nearer and nearer the city. The barbarians moved nearer too, in a vast arc that penned Mohenjo-Daro against the Indus flood. They neither hurried nor skulked; why should they? Nobody in the mud-brick warrens could stop them.

The stifling day wore slowly toward sundown. The water rose faster, breaking at last in ripples across the street pavements. This brought people crowding outside, fighting to climb onto trash-covered rooftops.

From there, at last, they saw the wide ring of strangers under the dust clouds, advancing calmly, axes and heavy swords ready.

The unarmed city dwellers stampeded then, in the only direction left to them—toward the booming Indus. Most waded in and disappeared after a time. But thirty-eight were too slow in leaving the higher part of the city. They never got out.

They ended, most of them, in the streets—reeling, staggering, thrashing, hacked wide and spouting red gouts, skulls split and emptying in the mud. Six were cut down in a lane—one of them a child. Twelve adults with another child were trapped inside a house and were butchered there. Two men and their wives, with five children, burrowed into a water-filled ditch, but the raiders saw them and chopped until all were dead. Four others were found hiding foolishly in a public bath; one was knocked over backwards as she tried to get upstairs to the street, another was drowned in the bath, and the others were clubbed just outside.

All these corpses were left where they lay, to tell their silent stories thirty-five hundred years later. The remaining six were tossed into a trench. Then the raiders finished their search, taking whatever pleased them or might be useful. But the loot probably disappointed them. Mohenjo-Daro had been poor and squalid for generations. The invaders had no desire to stay, with the stench of death in their noses and the muddy water at their knees.

They went away almost immediately. Far away. No later generation was sure who they were, because they never put down roots in the Indus basin or even in the Punjab.

In the nineteenth century the British found that whole region still barren and deserted. Like the Harappan people long before, they cut a new network of canals and irrigated and cultivated the land. It became a granary for the whole area, supporting one and a half million people by 1940.

Mohenjo-Daro vanished so completely under the mud that even the memory of it was lost. What had caused the decline that let it fall so limply?

No one had a simple answer. Many factors might have combined against it: thinning crops, racial inter-breeding, failures of leadership and morale, ecological imbalance.

The connections between deforestation, soil erosion, flooding, and "dust bowls" began to be understood only in this century. Five thousand years ago, forests may have mantled the hills bordering the Indus basin. Every tree would have been chopped down eventually, either for firewood or for use in the earliest buildings at Mohenjo-Daro. The structures of those first buildings showed that timbers, which later rotted away entirely, had originally reinforced many walls.

Rainfall could be heavy once in a decade or so, and could scour off tons of topsoil not protected by trees. Torrential runoff from the hills would have increased the flooding of the Indus. Dust from those treeless slopes would have worsened the dust storms.

Slow geologic changes, such as the lifting of an entire coastline or riverbed, could also have helped undo the empire. For example, evidence was found that certain places now thirty miles inland were once seaports on the coast of the Arabian Sea. If a river changed course or a port became useless, maybe vital commerce stopped reaching Mohenjo-Daro.

Most terrifying of all might have been a poisoning of land caused by a rise in the underground water table, which forced the salts of the earth to the surface and made croplands revert to desert. All those centuries of irrigation by the Mohenjo-Daro engineers might have waterlogged the land eventually, with the same results that are occurring there now. I saw them from an airplane.

Looking down on the Indus basin, I saw green fields splotched with gray decay like mildew on an old carpet—salty rime, patternless and ominous, erupting in disconnected patches here and there. It didn't spread predictably. It might wither a village in Gujrat one year, deprive Shahpur farmers of all livelihood the next. It was like some epidemic out of a science fiction novel.

The British Empire never learned to cure it, nor did the successor governments of India and Pakistan.

The British used to say that one or two cricket pitches were going under every day; recently the Punjabis found themselves losing at least 150 acres every afternoon. They might be reliving the decline of the Indus civilization.

The first chapters of the story of that ancient civilization will probably never be known, because a rising water table has hidden them. In 1950 archaeologists bored a hole below the lowest city levels they had excavated. Even though it was the driest part of the year, they struck water sixteen feet underground. With mechanized pumps and careful engineering they went down ten feet farther into the streaming mud. Then one night, while the pumps were laboring, a hundred jets of water burst from the sides of their cutting, and with a roar the hole caved in.

The diggers had gone deeper than any of their predecessors had, but time and tide had beaten them. They estimated that something like thirteen feet of waterlogged city—the earliest and perhaps the best—remained entirely unexposed. They saw no hope of ever excavating it.

The Indus Valley empire could be called prosaic in comparison with the richer and better-known civilizations of Egypt and Sumer. But much of its contribution could be unknown. Not knowing, I could feel the tragedy of its ending. A people had roused themselves from untold centuries of quiet existence in the mountains, and made a total effort in the strange and hazardous lowlands. They cleared the jungle, fought wild beasts, tamed the powerful river, planned and built their twin cities, and created a thriving civilization where there was only wilderness before and after them.

Who they were, where they came from, and where their few survivors went would never be known. Their gods, kings, heroes, thinkers, and artists were obliterated. When first visible to us they were already mature and highly developed, with their early struggles and failures unrecorded. All we know is that eventually they succeeded, and their toil produced a civilization that laid foundations for the rich culture of historic India.

# 14

# The First Civilization?

A student named Stephen Young, walking along a forest trail in 1966, tripped and fell. He found his fingers resting on new clues to where and how civilization began.

The clues had to do with bronze.

Bronze is common. You handle it when you pick up small change. And in doing so you touch the stuff of history, for bronze shaped much of history. In the so-called Bronze Age man put away stone tools and began practicing the arts and crafts of what we call civilization.

Nations might ascend to grandeur without writing, conceivably, and certainly without the wheel, but they couldn't very well function without fused metals, of which bronze was the first. As long as men used only stone and wood, they seemed condemned to a life of hunting and fishing. (We saw a few chapters ago that a Stonehenge civilization might have been an exception

—although I didn't see how Stone Age men could have known the world was round, and could have set out stones in patterns to solve quadratic equations.)

Around some unknown campfire, probably somewhere in western Asia, probably eight or ten thousand years ago, somebody made a discovery that changed the world—the discovery of metalworking. Like many of mankind's great discoveries, it may have been accidental.

Stone Age people had already learned to model clay pots and bake them. They used a kiln, or oven, to fire their products. They were venturing out in search of types of earth that might make better pottery. Maybe these searches turned up hunks of gold or copper in almost pure form. Or maybe metallic copper was found in the ashes of fires built on rocks containing copper ore.

Anyhow, people who were curious and were lucky enough to find these strange substances were bound to put them into a pottery kiln sooner or later, just to see what would happen. They undoubtedly were startled at the result.

The colored rocks behaved differently than flint or obsidian. Fire turned them liquid. When the fire cooled, the liquid resolidified, in the shape of whatever it was resting on. This new solid was soft enough to be hammered into a thin sheet with a stone, and its edge could be ground down.

Later, metalworkers discovered the art of smelting, or coaxing metals from rock by heating the stony ore in their kilns. Next they learned to pour molten copper or gold into a clay or sand mold to solidify. It was far easier to shape than rock, and it was ideal for ornaments because polishing gave it beautiful luster. Metals probably were made into ornaments for a thousand years before anyone put them to more mundane uses such as spearheads and axheads.

Copper, the oldest known metal to be adapted to human use, was discovered in Asia about 6000 B.C., in prehistoric Mesopotamia around 4500 B.C., in Egyptian graves toward 4000 B.C., in the ruins of Ur about 3100 B.C. Coppersmiths were prospering in the early city states of Mesopotamia around 3000 B.C. Maybe it was because eastern Mediterranean lands were rich in copper that strong cultures arose in Mesopotamia and Egypt, spreading to transform the world.

Copper was soft. It could be drawn into wire, handy for many purposes, and its pliability was useful in other ways. But it was too soft for tools or weapons; it needed an alloy to harden it. Sometimes people stumbled onto natural alloys—copper that nature had already mixed with tin or zinc to form ready-made bronze or brass—but many centuries may have passed before anyone thought of the next step: deliberate fusing of metals to make compounds, which were harder.

By adding one part of tin to nine of copper, metalsmiths got a substance much superior to copper or stone. It could be worked into sharper edges and points. It kept its cutting edge for a longer period of time. And it was durable enough to emerge only dented from a battering that would splinter a wooden club or shatter a stone ax. These advantages more than compensated for the fact that metal was heavier than stone and harder to find.

Archaeologists know that bronze making goes back at least five thousand years, for bronze was found in Minoan ruins of 3000 B.C., in Egyptian tombs of 2800 B.C., and in the Troy of 2000 B.C. Bronze gave the Indus Valley the first industrial cities, as we saw in the last chapter; moreover, the beautiful bronze statuette of a dancer from Mohenjo-Daro was dated about 2500 B.C.

There was a magic in this metal, which perhaps was more exciting than its practicality. Molten, it poured more easily than copper, yet it was harder; its color moved mysteriously from red-gold to deep green or soft azure with the passing of years; and not being a precious metal, it didn't prompt greed before admiration. It prompted love, inspiring much of the world's best sculpture and metalwork. It became common currency, and bronze coins have been with us ever since.

At last mankind had found a versatile metal—easy to forge, easy to cast, yet tough enough for daily use. With bronze a royal era commenced. The many-colored metal gleamed like copper and like the gold kept hidden in nobles' coffers for feast days. What was copper, or even gold, against this new substance? This was really the metal for monarchs: malleable and beautiful as gold, but much, much harder. Swords and bangles, daggers and clasps, and shields and belt buckles of bronze began to be traded across the world. Implements that gave men leisure to build civilization were spreading: razors, tongs, sewing needles, saws, mirrors, cooking pans, and countless other kinds of hardware.

It would be a good guess that the Bronze Age dawned first in regions with supplies of copper and tin. Among these were the Iberian peninsula and England, so it came about that Tuscany, Rome, Spain, and England were important in the early history of the Old World. But before their time, Bronze Age civilizations arose elsewhere.

The first, so far as the spades have shown, were in fertile Near East lands—especially in a huge crescent-shaped area between the Tigris and Euphrates rivers. The early Mesopotamian cultures arose there. Yet nobody could discover the source of tin for these civilizations. Even so, bronze was common about 3000 B.C. in Ur—the earliest known date for it anywhere, until young Young upset the archaeological timetable in 1966.

What his fingers found when he fell into the dirt that summer day was evidence that the first site of the Bronze Age might be in Thailand rather than in the Near East, and that it might date back as far as 4500 B.C.—a good fifteen centuries before bronze was known to be manufactured elsewhere.

Only after years of testing and controversy did archaeologists begin to admit that Young's chance discovery might really mean what it seemed to. Young, the son of a former U.S. ambassador to Thailand, happened to be in the village of Ban Chieng on a Harvard grant to study the political culture of villages in northeast Thailand. The place where he was hiking had recently been washed out by monsoon rains. This was why he tripped on a root, and why his hands happened to land on clay rings. They were tops of small burial urns interred vertically. They had lain in the soil for thousands of years, until the rains exposed them at last.

The pots were about the size and shape of large pineapples. These humble-looking vessels turned out to have been made about 4500 B.C., according to "thermoluminescent dosimetry" (TLD) analysis, a new test for dating pottery.

Older pottery existed elsewhere. But the Ban Chieng pots were exciting because they were found in graves that also contained bronze objects.

Science had no test to measure the age of bronzework. No matter. If the dates indicated by the testing of the burial urns were right, this implied that bronze in the same graves had been used in 4500 B.C. too.

Northern Thailand happened to be one of a few areas where both tin and copper were in adequate supply. The ores were rich enough for smelting by primitive methods. So the evidence added up. It suggested that people living in what is now Thailand were making bronze for their own use in 4500 B.C., and by 3000 B.C. might have been exporting the tin and know-how that the proclaimed "cradle of civilization" in the Near East needed for bronzemaking. In short, the world's first Bronze Age people conceivably lived in Thailand. Almost certainly they preceded those in Sumer.

Even when excited, the academic world seldom moves faster than a snail. So it wasn't until 1973 that Young's discovery evoked systematic digging at Ban Chieng. Then the scholarly burrowers turned up 115 prehistoric graves. These contained some five hundred pots—together with a number of bronze artifacts. The excavators were especially pleased to find bronze axheads with sandstone molds into which the axheads fit. Even nitpickers could scarcely argue that these axheads had been brought in by traders.

Professor Froehlich Rainey of the University of Pennsylvania is an eminent archaeologist; for many years he has written the annual entries on archaeology for the Yearbook of the Encyclopedia Britannica.

He went to Ban Chieng. In 1976 he told William H. Honan of *The New York Times:*

> After four separate, systematic excavations I can say that C-14 dates show that the mound at Ban Chieng was occupied between at least 3500 B.C. and 200 B.C., and that advanced bronze metallurgy was practiced there throughout that period. We're finding very old bronze virtually everywhere we look. It is technically advanced—cast in molds, with high tin content. When we find this we know there also has to be earlier and less sophisticated bronze—stuff that's almost pure copper, shaped by hammering.
>
> When this discovery is put together with the earliest pottery, which was found in Japan, and with seeds and rice husks found at a paleolithic site along the Thai-Burmese border, you have evidence that all the basic arts of civilization—agriculture, pottery and bronze making—may have begun in this part of the world. It seems to me we'll unquestionably demonstrate that advanced bronze manufacture is considerably older in the Far East than in the Near East.

What were they like, these bronze makers in Thailand? On such scanty evidence, no one could guess. But I went to take a look anyhow.

Where they had lived, an elegant civilization was known to have flourished many centuries later. It was the Khmer culture of Thailand and Cambodia. Maybe it was descended from the early Bronze Age culture there. Just maybe.

The Khmers' origin was uncertain, but it is known that they sprang from—or merged with—a misty nation known as Funan. From about 200 A.D. to about 550, Funan thrived. Then it became—or was superseded by—Khmer.

In time immemorial the Khmer people drew their culture from the Indian subcontinent, even though they were basically Chinese and partly Tibetan. (Could they have absorbed refugees from the obliterated Indus Valley civilization? This might explain their leanings toward India.)

There was plenty of evidence that Indian religion and art had advanced together across straits and frontiers into Thailand and Cambodia, perhaps rusticating quietly in jungle tribes before surfacing with the Khmers. Later, after about eight splendid centuries, Khmer civilization decayed and disappeared.

In 1858 the French explorer Henri Mouhot, inching his way through masses of vegetation in the upper valley of the Mekong River, saw an incredible vision: a majestic temple half strangled with flamboyant foliage but soaring triumphantly out of the trees and vines—a thousand tons of intricately carved masonry poised against the sky.

It spread away as far as he could see into the tangled jungle depths. He didn't know that he had found the temple-tomb of Angkor Wat, the finest achievement of the Khmer civilization, and the greatest of all temples anywhere, in the judgment of some temple fanciers.

Mouhot wondered later if he had really seen that overwhelming sight or had suffered a hallucination. So did his listeners when he returned to France. Cambodia was one of the most remote parts of the benighted heathen East. The nineteenth-century Western world never even dreamed that a civilization might have thrived in the enormous glooms of an Asian jungle. But Mouhot insisted that the ruins he had seen were "far more grandiose than anything built in the heyday of Greek or Roman art."

In 1604 a Portuguese missionary told of hunters reporting a giant ruin in the central Cambodian jungle, and another priest made a similar report in 1672, but no attention was paid. Not much attention was paid to Mouhot either, until other Europeans corroborated him. Then France took steps to make Cambodia a protectorate, and scientific expeditions hacked their way to the once-silent site. Soon Angkor Wat became one of the world's wonders.

Mouhot died of tropical fever, never knowing the

full significance of his discovery. He wrote: "One must imagine the most beautiful creations of architecture transported into the depths of the forests . . . the only remaining signs, alas, of a lost race."

If he could only know, he would be surprised and charmed to see how much of the glittering civilization was eventually reconstructed. Researchers pieced together evidence from many sources, much of it Hindu. India had been a marvel and a mystery to Europe, but diligent scholars were opening up Hindu thought and history like a new intellectual continent.

Even the imposing pyramidal structure of Angkor, like their many other temples, called *wats,* were Hindu-inspired, symbolizing a mountain home of gods. By the beginning of Europe's Christian era, Hindu law, literature, architecture, and sculpture had spread south and east to what became Burma, Thailand, Malaya, and the Indonesian Islands. In Cambodia the Funan kingdom, probably Chinese, was infiltrated by Hindu culture and ideals.

The Khmer kings, devout followers of Siva and Vishnu, needed many slaves and therefore waged many wars in Thailand and elsewhere. Their slaves and war captives built Angkor Wat, a structure so huge that several dozen Greek temples and the imperial palaces of Rome could all have fitted within it.

A vast artificial moat, twelve miles in circumference, six hundred feet wide, surrounded the temple. Over the moat ran a paved bridge balustraded with huge stone snakes; then an ornate enclosing wall; then galleries extending almost half a mile, studded with bas-reliefs of gods and kings and scenes from Hindu religious epics; then the imposing edifice itself, rising on a broad base through terrace after terrace by sweeping stone staircases that rivaled those of Versailles. On top was the sanctuary of the gods, two hundred feet high, and five watchtowers.

This was a fortified tomb and temple, for the exclusive habitation of gods and ghosts and possibly priests. Aristocrats had smaller palaces, and ordinary people dwelled in simple wood huts. Most of them worked in rice fields to the tinkle of temple bells, amid the soft scent of joss sticks mingled with the fragrance or orange and banana groves.

The cityscape was rich and carefully planned with canals and artificial lakes, good paved roads, and numerous small temples every mile or so. Every wall writhed with the movement of bas-reliefs.

Kublai Khan's ambassador, Chou tá-Kuan, visited the Khmer capital in 1206. He found a barefoot king gorgeously caparisoned in gold, ruling a nation that had generated massive wealth from rice paddies and slave labor. Pleasure boats dotted the lakes. Streets were thronged with curtained howdahs, chariots under parasols. Elephants in gilded harnesses. Tiny rainbows twinkled from jeweled rings on nobles' fingers. There were hospitals with nurses and physicians. Kublai Khan, learning that the ambassador estimated a population of a million people, decided not to make war.

The hospitals seemed strange, because to Hindus, who believe in reincarnation, the body is unimportant; sometimes it is cremated after death, sometimes left to rot. Only the soul counts. But perhaps by this time Buddhism had begun its eclipse of Hinduism in Khmer.

Siva and Vishnu had inspired the Khmers to raise temple after temple in the jungles, as if building were in itself an act of piety. The artisans carved fretwork and statuary as patiently as if they had all eternity. But the Khmer faith also set great store by improving the land. Custom may have required newly enthroned kings to build dams and reservoirs before they began their temples; to cut roads through the jungles and give virgin fields to the farmers.

Perhaps life became almost narcotically agreeable under the warm sun in the smiling fields and groves. The last great Khmer king retired to meditate, and became a Buddhist monk. Many of his subjects were likewise converted.

Buddhism, with its disregard for human struggle and mild acceptance of poverty, discouraged the monument-building mania that had perhaps sapped the nation's energy beyond recovery. No new building was erected at Angkor for two centuries before its fall. The French scholar Louis Finot observed, "The Khmer people accepted [Buddhism], one may believe, without repugnance, and willingly laid down the crushing burden of their glory."

The end came in the fifteenth century. Warlike Thai tribesmen had been migrating into the area for decades, robbing orchards and stripping temples. Finally the Buddha-king died. To escape Thai onslaughts, many priests and courtiers defected, and people began to flee the opulent city by the thousands. In time Angkor Wat lay empty. The Khmer civilization faded away like an opium dream.

Five centuries later, when Mouhot asked the jungle natives who had built the temples and the miles of stone-flagged avenues under the creepers, they had no ancestral memories. "These things built themselves," some said. Others murmured, "It is the work of giants."

Chou ta-Kuan had told his warlord of many books written by Khmers, but not a single page survived. Like us, they put perishable thoughts on perishable materials, and their immortals died with their civilization. Only sculpture and architecture showed us the glory of the Khmer achievement. Perhaps the stone buildings, so exuberant that they seemed the complete and powerful expression of a race, were testimony enough.

# 15

# The Invisible Machines

Looking out over a lifeless wasteland, I thought of something Oliver Cromwell said: "No one rises so high as he who knows not whither he is going." The thought came out of memory and hit me because it applied to me at that very moment.

Not knowing where I might go, I had set out to find whatever was understandable of lost civilizations. Now, having followed a winding trail back and back through five millennia, I found myself with an unexpected overview of those vanished empires. The trail had led me to a new perspective.

The perspective was in my mind's eye, of course. My corporeal eyes were squinting at some low mounds rising from a yellow-brown plain, and a tumbled disorder of broken bricks. These were the remnants of the long-lost biblical city Ur of the Chaldees, mentioned in the eleventh chapter of the Book of Genesis as the home of the first patriarch Abraham.

An idea had dawned on me: An invisible machine had once been at work here. Almost the same machine was designed and put together by someone in the jungles of Cambodia, by someone else in the Indus Valley badlands, by others near here in this famed fertile crescent of land where so many of the earliest cities arose. The idea of the machine also gave me a little clearer understanding of the religious zeal of lost civilizations, particularly those mentioned in the Holy Scriptures.

Forty years ago nobody knew where Ur lay, if indeed it had ever existed. In those years the Old Testament was widely regarded as a poetic recounting of garbled folklore, rather than as a historical narrative of the Israelite nation. But then Ur was found, farther back in the darkness of time than even the cities of Egypt. This and other discoveries in the ancient Near East began to reverse the tide of skepticism.

Today the ruins of Ur are one of many stops on the famous Baghdad railway. I took the train at Basra, near the Persian Gulf, and went clanking through 120 miles of hot and dreary wastes. When the train let me off and the noise of the wheels died away, I was surrounded by a vast silence as of a house in order. I seemed to stand in the middle of an enormous brown dish bisected by the gleaming line of the railroad track. But when I turned I saw a higher mound among the low ones in the distance.

It was the ziggurat of Ur, forerunner of the Tower of Babel.

As I hiked to it my spirits soared despite the smothering heat. Ur was probably the place, from all archaeological evidence so far, where man first refined the most sublime invention on earth—civilization itself.

It was where the machines I had postulated had begun their wondrous work. Even in ruins, Ur was a place I was eager to explore.

Here the wheel first rolled upon a gridwork of city streets. Here chieftains first created the military phalanx and the chariot, two seemingly omnipotent secret weapons of their day. Here writing was first scratched on clay tablets. From here, Josephus said, Abraham took arithmetic to Egypt.

The residents of Ur, and those who learned from them in other Sumerian cities, were self-taught architects and hydraulic engineers. They wrote epic poetry. They studied the stars. Their minds evolved basic ideas for education, philosophy, and medicine. Scientific lore that they had passed on to the Arabs would eventually help awaken medieval Europe.

It was here—not in Egypt or Babylon or Greece—that men first made systematic, rational laws to govern human behavior. They established a crude and fragmentary but recognizable democracy—as well as the brutal and now-familiar concept of empire. They built the earliest known true city (not counting little Jericho, which I'll get to soon).

Now, a city isn't an overgrown village. There were villages for untold centuries before the strange new machines made cities possible. We might find seeds of civilization in a primitive farmer's hut, but we could see the flowering only in a city.

As you read this, perhaps you're thinking I was heat-struck. "Machines" long before the steam engine or even the waterwheel? Where was my proof?

I would have to admit that no specimen of the machine could be found in archaeological digs. The reason it has evaded detection, despite masses of direct evidence, is that it was composed almost entirely of human parts.

Come with me through my train of thought. As we go, you'll recognize signposts from all the earlier chapters of this book.

To begin with, how did an ancient city differ from a village? Why did I think one civilized, the other not?

The distinction would be hazy in our era, but it wasn't in antiquity. A wall made the difference—a barrier behind which residents were secure. Without walls, people might never have grown civilized enough to build cities.

Villages had no walls because villagers usually didn't need much protection. When external dangers threatened, they ran away until the danger passed. If houses were destroyed, they could be rebuilt without much trouble. If crops were lost, more could be planted, or fish and game could be hunted, because virtually all village families were self-sufficient.

A farm village couldn't grow very large because soon it would shelter more farmers than the adjacent land could support. Latecomers would have to walk so far to their plots that they would move away and settle elsewhere. But a city could grow because most residents earned their livings in ways other than farming.

Cities couldn't have existed during the first 900,000 years or so of human life, when food gathering kept everyone on the move. Perhaps the first chance to settle down came when animals were domesticated. I would suppose this got started when the helpless young of slain beasts were spared and brought home as playthings for children. The miracle of reproduction multiplied a few pets into a herd.

Next, maybe as recently as ten thousand years ago, women made the greatest economic discovery of all—the bounty of the soil. While men hunted, women learned to dig edible roots, pluck fruit and nuts from trees, and collect honey, mushrooms, seeds, and natural grains.

We can only guess when and how people first saw the function of the seed and turned collecting into sowing. Even today some Australian tribes merely pick wild grain, without trying to separate the seeds and plant them; I saw Indian tribes in the Sacramento River valley who never advanced beyond this stage.

From all we know about human evolution, it would seem highly improbable that the small-group, open-space rovers called *Homo sapiens* could ever learn to live in cities. Why would self-sufficient herdsmen and farmers want to stay enclosed in sharp-cornered rectangular spaces, amid loud noises and bright lights, within earshot of hundreds of other people, mostly strangers?

The answer, if ever discovered, might help us cope with the urban instability that frightens us today. The first cities arose so recently, practically overnight on the evolutionary time scale, that we've hardly had a chance to get used to them. The switch from a world without cities to our present situation would take only the last page of a 150-page book, if mankind's story were compressed century-by-century into such a book.

At some unknown time and place, a village and its outlying neighbors found enough comfort and free time to invent a city. That place probably was where the Garden of Eden legend originated. It was a drab area where I now walked.

The people in Ur were Sumerians. About 2300 B.C., when their civilization was already at least twelve hundred years old, the Sumerians set down in writing their conception of how their own world had been created. They had heard it ancestrally. It was later echoed in the first chapter of Genesis: God divided the waters and let dry land appear. He let the earth bring forth herbs and grass, and flowers and trees, each yielding seed.

God did indeed divide waters to form the region between the Tigris and Euphrates rivers. The Bible called it Aram-Naharaim-Syria, which meant "between the two waters." Its Greek name was Mesopotamia, "land between rivers." Today it is Iraq.

When I looked at the silent Tigris and Euphrates I found it hard to believe that they had watered Sumer and nourished the Hanging Gardens of Babylon. And they really aren't the rivers that did so, because they follow different courses now. When Abraham lived at Ur it was a bustling riverfront city, with ships moored a hundred feet from where I walked. The Euphrates (now eleven miles away) spread phenomenally fertile silt, just as in the deltas of the Nile and the Indus.

This gave primitive Sumerians some spare time. A few concentrated on crafts they enjoyed. Specializing, they became more expert than the average rustic, who had to be his own carpenter, tailor, well-digger, boatbuilder, shoemaker, metalworker, and food supplier.

The new specialists produced things that farmers would travel miles for, bringing foodstuffs or skins in exchange. So as more specialists set up shop, a village grew larger, its marketplace boomed, more roads led to it, and it became well known. Displaying goods worth stealing (and perhaps artisans worth enslaving), it urgently needed defense. What to do?

Build a wall.

Even if heavily outnumbered by marauders, a walled community with food and water could feel safe. One man on a wall was worth several at its foot.

The earliest Egyptian symbol for "town" was a cross within a circle—a junction of roads inside a defensive wall. The difference between walled and unwalled settlements was so important that some archaeologists defined a "city" as "a settlement surrounded by a wall." The Greek word for city, *polis,* originally meant "citadel," and a citadel might consist of only a ring-wall.

Through tragic experience, some would-be cities found that their walls were too puny. If a city wall wasn't at least thirty feet high, attackers could surmount it with ladders. And if it wasn't at least fifteen feet thick, it didn't give defenders enough room to move along it and mass at threatened points.

Safe behind a good wall, people breathed more freely. Civic security and freedom were unheard-of blessings at first—so rare that cities were great wonders, and people flocked into them. Cities might become crowded but residents didn't leave. Medieval Germans probably spoke for civilized folk of many past centuries with their saying, "City air makes one free."

Even when the freedom was mostly illusory, people stayed. So the new idea of cities spread fast and far, relatively speaking.

At each city site, the wall problem had to be solved first. Even before mortar was invented, small stones made a wall that stood up to the weather better than baked mud—but enemies needed only to pry out a few stones, and whole sections tumbled down.

Therefore, many early fortifiers made walls of the very biggest rocks they could find. They trimmed them to fit roughly together, and stopped up chinks by pounding in small stones or packing them with mud.

The sheer weight of the rocks kept foes from pulling them out, especially if defenders were pelting them with missiles or raining down hot liquids.

Here we come to the invisible machine that I concluded was essential.

Power machinery was sometimes needed to move much bigger rocks than any ordinary motor truck could carry today; to grind and chip them into shape; to hoist and maneuver them precisely. So the machinery was created.

Unless we believe in supernatural forces or a hidden corps of superbeings, we must visualize this machinery as a disciplined assemblage of men. Its only lifeless parts, probably, were levers and inclined planes, and perhaps logs used as rollers.

Such a machine could concentrate enormous energy and accomplish previously unimaginable feats. I don't think I am playing with words when I classify a disciplined mass of people as a machine. The heavyweight thinker Lewis Mumford elaborated this idea as long ago as 1934 in his book *Technics and Civilization.*

"Machine" is defined in dictionaries as "any combination of interrelated parts for using or applying energy to do work." By this definition the machine that built the walls of Ur and so many other early cities was a true machine—all the more mechanical because the human bodies that were its moving parts had become what modern technologists would call servomechanisms—virtual robots, totally obedient.

What induced a crowd of people to dehumanize themselves for months or years of preplanned labor? I think it was a powerful belief in something beyond themselves. In a word, religion.

Some genius discovered this way of establishing feelings of solidarity among thousands of persons. It was a task for an expert, a full-time specialist. Paul Wheatley of the University of Chicago, studying ancient cities, concluded that "specialized priests were among the first to be released from the daily round of subsistence labor."

These priests exhorted other people needed for the building of walls and temples. They sold the idea of enhancing the glory of high-born individuals close to the gods. Probably they also sold visions of what a city could mean to the city dwellers themselves. It could mean more abundance and more leisure someday, and could free everyone from the dull village grind.

The toilers might even see themselves as purchasing an earthly paradise; without walls there could be no paradise. (The very word *paradise,* in the original Persian, meant "walled garden.") They probably cherished hopes of order, beauty, and human fellowship. Why not? Behind walls they did create the beautiful ideas and art that comprised civilization.

But it turned out that countless workers passed their whole lifetimes in the human machine. The wall was only the beginning of their toil. Public works and public utilities were essential even for a small city like Ur. Canals had to be cut, wide fields irrigated, crops threshed, streets paved, waterworks built.

Someone planned this. Maybe committees did it in Ur and Mohenjo-Daro and Zimbabwe, but I couldn't imagine it, knowing something about the ways of committees. A supreme Big Brother was more likely. And in fact he was found to exist in every ancient city where detailed records came to light: a king revered as divine. The village's hunter-chieftain became a monarch and god when he built a city.

Minos, Theseus, the pharaohs, and countless kings and sultans and potentates acted in the name of a god when they created their cities. Each king's first act, the very key to his authority, was to put up a temple. Then he erected a wall around the temple and his followers, turning the whole area into a sacred place: a city.

A king's power to make decisions could be good for his people. A large population, acting as one, could bring about vast public improvements, far beyond the scope of villages. Unlike a village council of elders, a king could make decrees that would change the environment or the people's behavior.

But his power was precarious unless his people worshiped him.

Without this religious fervor, it seemed to me,

people wouldn't have done much more than erect the city walls. But they went on to build pyramids and ziggurats and tombs—Angkor Wat and Stonehenge and Knossos and many others. I would guess that every prehistoric complex of stone buildings was the home of a supposed god.

This was the other big reason, probably, why people liked to live in cities. To inhabit the same city as a god was to be "out of this world," so to speak. It was to be a member of a supercommunity. The idea could captivate even distant villages; they made pilgrimages to the city on religious festival days.

Every society has an image of itself, its way of life. In ancient times, kings and priests shaped this image. The medieval Christian image of heaven as a place where the blessed found their highest fulfillment in beholding God and singing his praises was only a slightly etherealized version of how a city like Ur seemed to its residents. Even in the comparatively late Etruscan culture, when a new city was founded, a priest held the plow that traced the outlines of the wall to be built.

A king not only played God but provided a satisfying life for his subjects. They shared vicariously in his triumphs of hunting, warfare, amorous conquest, or whatever. He also had to keep them busy—so he decreed the building of temples, tombs, and monuments. People could get joy from such labor. The great European cathedrals were built by voluntary toil through centuries.

What kept people busy in Ur? Mostly the brick mountain rising from an ocean of dust, toward which I was walking.

It was the Ziggurat of the Moon God Nannar. Sir Leonard Woolley had excavated and partially restored it in the 1930s. He wrote:

> The ziggurat is a peculiar feature of Sumerian architecture which can now be traced back to the earliest times. . . .
>
> The immigrants to lower Mesopotamia found themselves on a vast level plain where there was

no hill on which god could be properly worshiped. In every town which was big enough to warrant the effort the inhabitants built a "high place," a tower rising in stages, crowned by the town's principal shrine. This was the ziggurat.

Of them all, the biggest and most famous was, in course of time, the Ziggurat of Babylon, which in Hebrew tradition became known as the Tower of Babel. It was but a repetition on a slightly larger scale of the ziggurat of Ur, and it too was built by Ur-Nammu.

Ur-Nammu was one of the last Sumerian kings. His stone mountain set a fashion among civilizations for two thousand years. It was a three-stage pyramid, each step a broad terrace, inset with a winding external stairway. I climbed to the lofty height where the city's patron divinity Nannar might dwell. His one-room sanctum was paved with blue enameled tiles and paneled with rare woods like cedar and cypress, inlaid with marble, onyx, alabaster, agate, and gold.

This temple, like so many that followed, had been more than just a monument. It was a holy place, tended and cared for every day. Hymns and prayers were composed and recited there. Rites were planned and performed. Sacred festivals were celebrated. So a specialized priesthood proliferated. The temple and its coterie naturally became the intellectual center. Writing was invented and practiced in the temples, and probably arithmetic too.

Poor as well as rich turned over to the temples whatever share of worldly goods they thought would be sufficiently pleasing. The priests couldn't personally spend or consume the wealth that flowed in, so they became the city's financiers, investing in profitable-looking ventures such as trade missions elsewhere. They also became money changers and money lenders to the citizenry. Sometimes they lent to the sick or poor without interest, merely asking a return of the principal when the gods became more beneficent. Gods weren't aloof from men; some of them lived on earth in the temples, ate heartily, and augmented the population through communion with pious women.

Building the ziggurat was the great labor to which Ur-Nammu consecrated masses of willing manpower. Earlier there had been other big jobs. The outer wall had been first and biggest. "It was colossal and must have seemed to the builder impregnable," Sir Leonard Woolley wrote. "But it was to fall in the end. Not a trace remained. . . . Just because the defenses of Ur had been so strong the victorious enemy dismantled them systematically, leaving not one brick upon another."

As I clambered down from the ziggurat I mused about the patriarch Jacob. His grandfather had told him of this great building at Ur with stairs up to heaven —such was indeed the name of Nannar's shrine. Perhaps he subconsciously recalled this when he dreamed, as told in the twenty-eighth chapter of Genesis, of ladders (or staircases, the word is the same) up to heaven.

Down in the sand and rubble, I imagined Ur as it had been, with a busy bazaar—not much different, Sir Leonard Woolley said, from Near Eastern bazaars today. I might be wandering through narrow streets shadowed by awnings and lined with booths. For food I could choose from onions, cucumbers, dates and apples and other fruit, dried fish, pork, duck, mutton, cheeses, and spices. The crush of noisy people was bothersome; blind beggars plucked at me from all sides. "The poor are always with us," the Sumerians were fond of saying.

On the imaginary bazaar stands I saw ivory combs from India and carnelian beads from Persia. This little city earned a good income by sending history's first traveling salesmen clear down the Persian Gulf to Harappa and Mohenjo-Daro in the Indus basin, and far up the valleys of the Euphrates and Tigris into Turkey and Kurdistan. It had a managed economy under the king's rule, bolstered by his immense practical contributions in creating collective wealth, and distributing, not an equal share but a "fair share" to everyone, even the beggars.

Ur was a sort of dictatorship, as all ancient cities

probably were, but it was an oddly appealing society. Slaves bought their freedom, married, fought court cases. Children argued with teachers. Ombudsmen kept trivial disputes out of the courts. Taverns offered pleasure-bent citizens the Sumerian equivalents of "wine, women and song."

This was civilization as mankind first knew it, apparently. The term was and is hard to define. Sometimes people said "civilized" when they meant kind, honest, or considerate—but these attributes were often found in primitive people too. To etymologists, "civilized" originally meant "living in cities." Later it meant giving loyalty to a community instead of just to a clan or tribe.

At any rate, civilization was based on religion. This was clear in biblical accounts of Sumer, Babylonia, Assyria, Egypt, and Israel, the kingdoms that arose in the two-thousand-year span of the Old Testament.

Our own generation was startled to learn how much in the Old Testament was true. Take the seemingly allegorical tale of Noah's Ark and the Flood. Evidence had turned up that Ur could have been the location of such a story. This was another reason why I was deeply curious about the place.

Hardly an ancient people was without folklore of a flood. The familiar Bible story wasn't originally Hebrew at all. The Hebrews got it from Sumer and wove it into their own sacred canon with suitable emendations. The earlier tale was on tablets written before Abraham's time and found in ruins of the library at Nineveh. They recounted the first epic known to literature, at least fifteen centuries prior to Homer: the epic of the mighty folk hero Gilgamesh, king of the ancient city of Uruk. (The Bible too mentioned Uruk. Excavations revealed its ziggurat and a library of thirty thousand clay tablets near Ur.) In this story King Gilgamesh met the survivor of a huge flood, whose story was so like the Bible's—even in wording—that the writers of Genesis must have used a common source.

This parallel didn't necessarily confirm the story, of course. But when Sir Leonard Woolley excavated Ur he found an eleven-foot layer of silt sandwiched between strata of successive civilizations. "Eleven feet of silt would probably mean a flood not less than twenty-five feet deep," he reported. "In this flat low-lying land a flood of that depth would cover an area about three hundred miles long and a hundred miles across. The whole fertile land between the Elamite mountains and the high Syrian desert would disappear, every village would be destroyed. . . . It was not a universal deluge; it was a vast flood in the valley of the Tigris and Euphrates which drowned the whole of the habitable land between mountains and desert; for the people who lived there that was all the world. The great bulk of those people must have perished. If some household managed to escape by boat from the drowned lowlands, the head of it would naturally be hero of the saga."

Utnapishtim, the Noah of the Bible story, described weather conditions seen in Iraq and thereabouts in modern times. He expressly mentioned a southern gale; the Persian Gulf, whose waters were shoved across the flat country by the gale, lay south of the Tigris-Euphrates estuary. To the last detail, the black clouds, howling noise, sudden darkness, and terrible wind were characteristic of a cyclone. In 1876 a cyclone of this kind swept a tidal wave across the Bay of Bengal, headed for the coast at the mouth of the Ganges, then covered 141 square miles inland with fifty feet of water, drowning 215,000 people.

It seemed that Sir Leonard Woolley had found the historical reality behind the Flood legend. He himself said that what convinced him was a king list drawn up by Sumerian scribes soon after 2000 B.C., a sort of skeleton outline such as we see in textbooks. The list was divided into kings "before the flood" and "after the flood." Obviously a flood had broken the continuity of the kingdom's history. Sumerian schoolboys evidently knew of just one flood—what we would call Noah's Flood. It was no fable.

Another Bible story of the Near East also intrigued me: the tale of Jericho, the oldest walled town known to archaeology, whose walls reportedly fell flat when the besieger Joshua blew his trumpet. Could this be possible?

Jericho and Ur lay at opposite tips of a great crescent of fertile soil that curved around the Persian Gulf and the Arabian Desert. Ur was in the corner of southern Mesopotamia. Jericho was far west in the Jordan River valley, nine miles from the north end of the Dead Sea. It was bordered by barren hills, but at Jericho itself springs nourished trees and grass, making an oasis in the hot parched land.

By digging down sixty feet, archaeologists determined that the site of Jericho had been inhabited from about 9000 B.C. until about 1325 B.C., when the Israelites razed it. In 1600 B.C. it was a thick-walled town of about two thousand people, fairly civilized and settled, to judge from funerary offerings found in tombs of its kings. The chief digger, Professor John Garstang, said the testimony of the ruins confirmed the Bible story. I had to see this.

I approached from the west rim of the Jordan valley, as Joshua and his Israelites had. I looked down through the shimmering heat toward a maze of houses and alleys, the present-day Jordan. In the far distance, beyond the valley plain, I could see the low mountains of Gilead and Moab, and the Mediterranean, a dark streak beyond the white dunes. This was how Moses saw it before he died: "The Lord showed him all the land . . . unto the utmost sea." (Deuteronomy 34)

Descending, I found myself on the edge of a barren waste of chalk, not far west of the river. This would have been the place to ford the narrow muddy Jordan, on its way into the Dead Sea.

The modern village was surrounded by a cluster of green palms with golden-red clusters of dates. But the ancient town wasn't accessible. The site of the excavations lay behind a barbed-wire fence, and I had to buy a ticket to see it.

It was a wide, deep hole, like the excavation for a large building. Under the strata of the Bronze Age, at the bottom, lay cross sections of what had been put down in the Stone Age when people first built dwellings. I saw the foundations of round walls seven thousand years old; those early inhabitants evidently modeled their houses on the round tents of the desert nomads.

The most fascinating remainders were those of the famous walls of Jericho, buried for thousands of years but now standing out clearly. These were walls the patriarchs had seen.

They were built partly of great boulders, like so many city walls that followed them. A thirty-foot watchtower (its massive mud-brick foundations still visible, showing the internal stairway) dominated the walls. The walls encircled an area of about eight acres, the size of St. Peter's Square in Rome. Compared with Ur this town was tiny, but it was one of the strongest forts in Palestine (or Canaan, as the Promised Land was called).

Looking at the foundations, I thought this fort must have seemed impregnable. It was double-walled. The outer of the two concentric rings, made of mud bricks, was about thirty feet high and six feet thick. After climbing it or breaking through, attackers would be on the ground again, confronting a higher and thicker inner wall set into a hill. Had Joshua really shaken down those two walls?

They were down now. The space between where they had stood was filled with blackened rubble, charred bricks, ashes, cracked stones. Obviously there had been a fierce fire. The Bible said, "They burnt the city with fire and all that was therein."

The foundations were cracked here and there. What cracked them? As he dug, Garstang made a discovery that told the amazing story. The stones of the outer wall lay in places that showed they had fallen outward and downhill—but the inner wall had fallen inward, burying buildings that nestled at its base.

This pointed to only one explanation, Garstang said. An earthquake must have shaken down the walls. Jericho lies in the Great Rift, an earthquake fault zone running from Tibet down through the Red Sea and into eastern Africa.

For seven days, the Bible said, the children of Israel marched around the walls, striking terror into the hearts of the inhabitants. But the fort resisted all attacks. And then an earthquake struck, perhaps at almost the moment Joshua happened to be blowing his trumpet for another charge. If the Israelites saw this as divine intervention on their behalf, who could gainsay them?

# 16

# Old Enemies

You can pack only so much into a television show, because of time limitations. You can tell more in a book, but again there are limits, of space.

If I had enough space I'd write about the riddle of Easter Island, an isolated speck in the South Pacific where stone statues as tall as three-story houses gaze sternly out to sea. Some of the statues weigh a hundred thousand pounds. All were carved so symmetrically that when they were erected they balanced perfectly. Calculating how many people were needed to carry them several miles over jagged volcanic terrain, you have to believe that such an army could reach Easter Island only by repeated, planned voyages; a few dozen castaways didn't lift those rocks. Who did it, and why? I wish we knew.

I also wish I had room to write about Bactra, a Greek city in Afghanistan established by Alexander the

Great. Its twenty-two-mile wall must have enclosed a teeming population, but now its ruins lie half buried in sand. And I wish I'd seen Çatal Hüyük in the Konya plain of southern Turkey. Five thousand people lived there in one immense blockhouse of a city; when they went home, they climbed a ladder, walked over the roofs until they reached their own apartments, then went down into the bosoms of their families by way of the chimneys. In those apartments are the oldest known wall paintings, dating back eight thousand years. There are also bulls' horns ceremoniously arranged in a way that is remarkably suggestive of the "horns of consecration" atop the palace at Knossos. "It is a long jump from Asia Minor in 6500 B.C. to Crete in 2000," wrote Professor M. I. Finley, ancient-history specialist at Cambridge University, "but this new find, taken together with all the other known links, cannot be dismissed as meaningless coincidence."

There were other ghost cities I'd have liked to cover: Nan Matal, called "the Venice of the South Seas," where the ruins of ninety great buildings show a unique architectural style; the mysterious skyscraper cities of the Hadhramaut Valley in Arabia; the unnamed, massive stone ruins somewhere in the Brazilian jungle, where legends say a civilization built cities long before the Incas—a civilization from a vanished continent like Atlantis. Colonel Percy H. Fawcett, a famed British explorer, found the city, came out to report on it, then headed back to examine it further, and was never heard from again.

If I had enough space I'd write a full chapter about my own journeys along black cliffs, dizzy with fathomless space below and above, leaning against winds that sometimes rose to a moan and made my clothes flutter like a ghost's shrouds. I was in the Andes, tracing almost-forgotten empires. The Inca and pre-Inca peoples built massive citadels there, like condors' nests, at inaccessible heights. Yet their walls encircled regular blocks of streets, as well as temples and altars and places to observe the rising and setting of the Sun God. They used thousands of huge stone blocks, beautiful in their mortarless, ingenious interlocking. Again, powerful machines of massed humanity had presumably been at work.

The Andes civilizations discovered and cultivated the potato. They used the seed, leaves, and roots of the aloe. They enriched crops with fertilizers. They made maize flour, bread, drink, and honey. All these could have come before they reached the city-building, temple-building stage that was the mark of ancient civilization. Then they dug networks of irrigation canals in the mountains. They smelted, welded, and soldered metals. They developed notable surgical and dental skill with bronze scalpels, copper wire, and gold inlays.

There are no folk tales in Peru telling how the great walled communities came or why they were abandoned. Did the Spaniards know of these places? Maybe. Their colonial archives contain only brief, vague references to something up there among the peaks. Did the residents perish of a plague? Or did they simply die of hunger and age? I could envision the last aging handful and then the last human being among the dead. But maybe it wasn't that way. Maybe the people just walked down into the lowlands. Maybe they were wiped out in war.

If this book could be bigger I'd write a chapter about my days in the sweltering Central American jungle, where sweat from my hands blurred what I wrote in my notebook. I saw flowers as big as faces, leaves like bodies, stems like human legs; this pulpy green world seemed almost to be a silent, crowded royal court. I knew there had been royal courts in these twilight solitudes a thousand years ago. I saw their spectacular stoneworks. And I pondered an old, unanswered query of the archaeologists: Why had a beardless race dreamed of bearded gods?

Before Columbus, before Erikson, before bearded adventurers from Europe ever dreamed of this unknown continent, Mayan frescoes and carvings portrayed gods with beards. Somehow the Mayas acquired a great store of knowledge—which they transmitted from city to city quickly and precisely. When their astronomers in Copán standardized the lunar calendar toward the end of the seventh century A.D., it was soon adopted in stone-carved chronologies across the Mayan world from the Gulf of Mexico to today's Nicaragua.

No Hindus, Greeks, or Romans plotted the paths of celestial bodies as meticulously as the Mayas did. They predicted eclipses of sun and moon. They calculated the path of elusive Venus, by turns morning and evening star, with an error of only fourteen seconds a year. They used elaborate systems of writing and computing, and even discovered the idea of *zero* eight hundred years ahead of Asia and Europe.

They were master architects, engineers, builders, and city planners, creating at least eighty majestic and geometric stone cities, some with temples two hundred feet tall. Their grand metropolis Tikal covered fifty square miles and housed forty thousand people, protected by surrounding earthworks. But they never discovered—or at least never used—metal, beasts of burden, the wheel, or the arch. They seldom cut windows in their buildings, leaving interiors dark and clammy.

Like the other early civilizations, they were obsessed with divine or magical forces. Their priest-aristocrats were hereditary rulers who monopolized knowledge and power. They kept the populace busy with insatiable building programs and a superhuman drive for height; steep-sided, temple-crowned pyramids like Mesopotamian ziggurats towered out of the jungle wherever the Mayas established cities.

I would have liked, also, to include a chapter about the shadowy Olmec civilization, the oldest in Central America and perhaps a parent of the Mayas. The Olmecs built jungle cities near Mexico's Gulf Coast as long ago as 1000 B.C. The region was low and hot—but rainy. How it rained! It came down in tons and avalanches. Jungles were crushed under the warm water and grew up to be crushed again. The total rainfall was 120 inches per year. The Mayan name for the region, Tamoanchan, meant "Land of Rain."

How could civilizations thrive for half a millennium or longer in such unfriendly environments as those that hemmed in the Mayas and the Olmecs? They could easily have chosen less jungly, swampy, insect-plagued regions; they brought huge basalt boulders for their idols and monuments from pleasanter areas at least eighty miles outside their domain. They might have put their cities where their basalt was. But maybe the massed human enterprises required to move forty-ton stones for many miles through dense vegetation were part of the mystique that created civilizations and kept them well oiled.

I wondered where these prehistoric civilizations of Central and South America came from. Man wasn't native to the New World. No bones such as Java man or Peking man, nor any apelike primates from which man evolved, were ever found there. In fact no apes at all, living or fossil, were found in the Americas.

Anthropologists said that remote ancestors of the New World people must have evolved in the Old World and migrated to America during the last stage of the Ice Age. Their supposed route was from Siberia across the Bering Strait and Alaska, then gradually down into North and South America, branching off as they went.

Perhaps so. Eskimos definitely came to this continent over the Bering Strait at a relatively recent date. But for the Incan, Mayan, Olmec, and other advanced civilizations in Latin America, such a long trek through extremes of climate and topography must have been fantastically hard. Did they take some easier route, now nonexistent? Unlike Eskimos and the Indians of North America, these civilizations were already highly developed when they first appeared here. It seems that they materialized out of nowhere, like Arabian jinns.

This is why some people theorize that a land bridge or at least a chain of islands once stretched from Peru or Chile to Easter Island and on through the Pacific. If the theory is correct, the land bridge has now sunk hundreds of fathoms, if we can trust oceanography experts, who say the bed of the Pacific is very deep. Still, a long lost continent in the Pacific, like theoretical Atlantis in the Atlantic, might solve this mystery of the brown-skinned breeds' arrival in unpopulated Latin America.

Their breakdown was even more puzzling. The Olmecs might have been absorbed into the Mayas. But the Mayas simply abandoned their own cities—some almost overnight, it seems—in the ninth century A.D. Buildings clearly in mid-construction were deserted. A great population, numbering in the millions after living and prospering in the jungles for seven centuries, seems to have dissolved into the undergrowth.

As far as we know, neither Mayas nor Incas had any contact with other cultures. Did they degenerate through inbreeding and cultural exhaustion brought about from having done the same things in the same ways for too long? I thought their disappearance would have been less sudden in that case. Were they suddenly attacked and overcome by enemies, as other civilizations were? Unlike those others, the Mayas rarely built walls to protect their cities; they might have thought that the jungle was wall enough, or that no enemies existed—only to discover in the end that they were mistaken.

A great earthquake like the one that devastated Guatemala in 1976 might have driven the Mayas mad with panic, though it obviously didn't shake down their stone pyramids. If these people had never heard of earthquakes, the first one might have stampeded them into the jungle, to die and rot there. Or a major hurricane might have had such effect.

Sumer and the Indus Valley civilization collapsed when the water table rose to the roots of their crops and killed them. The Mayan culture too might have fallen victim to a devastating crop disease, or human disease. Medical evidence indicates that Mayas shrank in stature, perhaps through malnutrition, in the final centuries of their long history.

But the most plausible explanation, many experts think, is that there was a revolt of the masses. The mighty human machine that had moved so many huge stones, built so many ceremonial centers, could have gone berserk and destroyed whoever controlled it, then wrecked itself.

Professor Alfred Kidder II, an eminent authority on preconquest America, wrote:

> Once embarked on a course of worship and propitiation involving great monuments and the work of numerous craftsmen, no leader . . . could afford to relax.
>
> Enough mistakes could lead a people under tension to revolt. If a cycle of drought, upsetting the crops, coincided with priestly predictions of good times and continued demand for labor, the people might have overcome their awe and destroyed the hierarchy in a day.

Professor Alfredo Barrera Vasquez agreed. "The Maya collapse is a clear-cut matter for me," he told a reporter in 1975. "At a certain point the demands of the aristocracy became unbearable. The people rebelled. Their only weapon was their overwhelming numbers. They probably strangled most of the overlords with their bare hands."

The rise and fall of the Mayas show man's capacity for greatness and his terrible affinity for doom. Isn't this true of the other ancient civilizations I had probed? Again and again, an elite of master builders, organizing a horde of docile human beings, sought to honor gods with mighty monuments—and ended, long centuries later, in ruin and limbo.

Something about enormous concentrations of people, with population pressures and many kinds of tension, transformed religion from a matter of simple rituals at village shrines to the great systems of temples and priesthoods invariably associated with early cities.

So those cities were paradoxes. In one sense they freed man, in another they enslaved him. The forces that transformed a humble human community into a gigantic collective work of art, exalting the spirit, also debased or wiped out precious human traits that the lowliest village cherished.

"Man," John Burroughs wrote, "is like the trainer of wild beasts who, at his peril, for one instant relaxes his mastery over them. Gravity, electricity, fire, flood, hurricane, will crush or consume him if his hands are unsteady or his wits tardy." It is true that some civilizations were obliterated by elemental forces; these were ancient enemies that threatened man a million years ago, and will threaten as long as mankind survives. But the wildest, most dangerous beasts were and are another species of enemy altogether: man himself.

Mother Nature never organized for the deliberate purpose of destroying man. Her attacks often strengthened him and sharpened his brain. He learned to prepare against drastic heat and cold, violent storms, and cyclic droughts. Sometimes his collective foresight fell short; cities withered because of centuries of ignorant misuse of forests and soil; others were buried in the boiling mud of volcanic upheavals, or drowned by rising water.

However, if natural forces were mankind's worst enemies, most of our lost civilizations would still be alive and well. Instead, they died when an old shadow, a monstrous growing shadow, fell across their walls. It was merely man—the other face of that nature that man always feared.

The simple wielder of sling and club had grown large enough to shadow the sun. When man learned to organize so he could build cities, he also made himself the cities' most dangerous foe.

Man the Organizer, Man the Propagandist, led whole civilizations up a dark pathway, dying often and blindly for some vision they could scarcely imagine. Lurking within every "civilized" leader were manias he never understood. In his pyramiding technological society, which esteemed outward aspects most highly, he undervalued his fellow man.

In religious texts chronicling the creation of cities, nothing struck me harder than the fierceness of god-kings toward one-another.Their murderous aggression, their moral blindness, and their greed and cruelty became means of manifesting divine power. Almost from the beginning, a god's labor machine was a war machine too. To destroy rival cities and abase rival gods became ends in themselves. Destructive fantasies that maddened totalitarians in our own age, from Hitler to Idi Amin, were common to the natures of the "divinely appointed" founders of the first civilizations.

When there were no rivals—as in the Mayan and

Incan and Indus Valley civilizations, at least for a while—the authoritarian system devoured itself. The great forces set in motion by the Organizer called for commensurately great collective enterprises. The human machines had to operate in a big way or they wouldn't work at all; no Boss, however big his bureaucratic apparatus, could govern a hundred little enterprises with their own craft skills, their own pride and quirks. Therefore, the machines were impersonal, if not dehumanized, by their very nature, and the planners developed the habit of "thinking big."

The superhuman pyramid building and dam building and palace building reduced the size and importance of the humans involved except for the central figure, the regal priestly Organizer himself. He knew he must keep the people worshiping him; once his royal power was switched off, his huge human machine either "went dead" or went wild. To keep power he had to seem able to see the future. Hence the enormous pains taken by priesthoods so that they could awe the populace by foretelling eclipses and solstices.

But even in the shadow of the pyramids the old cooperative ways and diverse thinking of the villages crept in and found niches, despite all Mr. Big could do. There had to be families and neighborhoods. There had to be a mixture of vocations, and a few independent craftsmen. There had to be a marketplace. So, even though it took centuries if not millennia, independent thinking filtered through the community. And ultimately the people went into the citadel and hacked the priests to death, or strangled them, or frightened them into fleeing.

Wherever this happened, civilization disintegrated and cities emptied. Leaderless and disorganized, the people disappeared in the mists of time.

But in a sense they had transcended themselves. They had risen above superstition and robot obedience. If only they had gone further, had learned to organize for their own good as well as that of whatever gods they revered!

Not knowing the past, they were condemned to repeat it, as George Santayana said. They had no way of knowing why other civilizations perished. Our generation was the first to know, even in dim outline.

Will our knowledge show us how to make our story a finer one? We have a great civilization to save or to lose. Those dead civilizations challenge us and we need the challenge.

Man isn't complete. Ancient brutish traits still lurk within him, but he is learning to outgrow them, I think. However gigantic or sacred our buildings may be, we are beginning to see that true civilization must be achieved in individual hearts. Looking back at those splendid but ultimately tragic ruins in deserts and jungles, maybe we'll see how to create the sublime society for which most of us have always yearned.

# BIBLIOGRAPHY


Al-Bakri, *Book of Roads and Kingdoms,* translated by J. R. Patterson. London: Routledge & Kegan Paul, 1930.

Archaeological Institute of America, *Archaeological Discoveries in the Holy Land.* New York: Crowell, 1967.

Barclay, William, *The Bible and History.* New York: Abingdon, 1968.

Bibby, Geoffrey, "Before the Argo," *Horizon,* July 1960.

Bloch, Robert, *The Etruscans.* London: Thames & Hudson, 1961.

Botsford, George W. and Robinson, Charles A. Jr., *Hellenic History.* New York: Macmillan, 1969.

Bowra, C. M., *Classical Greece.* New York: Time-Life Books, 1965.

——, "Homer's Age of Heroes," *Horizon,* January 1961.

*Cambridge Ancient History.* New York: Cambridge University Press, 1924.

Churchill, Winston, *My African Journey.* New York: George H. Doran, 1908.

——, *The Birth of Britain.* New York: Dodd, Mead, 1956.

Collingwood, R. C., *Roman Britain.* Oxford: Oxford University Press, 1937.

Cottrell, Leonard, *The Bull of Minos.* New York: Holt Rinehart & Winston, 1961.

——, *Lost Worlds.* New York: Doubleday, 1962.

Coughlan, Robert, *Tropical Africa.* New York: Time-Life Books, 1966.

Cloete, Stuart, *The African Giant,* New York: Doubleday, 1954.

Crampton, Patrick, *Stonehenge of the Kings.* London: Baker, 1967.

Davidson, Basil, *African Kingdoms.* New York: Time-Life Books, 1966.

——, "Africa: The Face Behind the Mask," *Horizon,* March 1963.

DeCamp, L. Sprague, *Great Cities of the Ancient World*. New York: Doubleday, 1972.

Durant, Will, *Our Oriental Heritage*. New York: Simon & Schuster, 1935.

——, *The Life of Greece*. New York: Simon & Schuster, 1939.

——, *Caesar and Christ*. New York: Simon & Schuster, 1944.

Eliot, Alexander, *Greece*. New York: American Heritage, 1972.

Evans, Sir Arthur, *The Palace of Minos*. London: Macmillan, 1921.

Fairservis, W. A. Jr., "Harappan Civilization: New Evidence and More Theory," *Novitates* (American Museum of Natural History), November 17, 1961.

Finley, M. I., *The World of Odysseus*. London: Macmillan, 1956.

Frazer, Sir James George, *The Golden Bough*. New York: Macmillan, 1951.

Gonzalez, Arturo F. Jr., "Lost Island of Atlantis?" *Science Digest*, May 1972.

Graham, Janet, "Are These the Walls of Camelot?" *Science Digest*, March 1968.

Hadas, Moses, *Imperial Rome*. New York: Time-Life Books, 1965.

Hale, William Harlan, *Ancient Greece*. New York: American Heritage, 1965.

Hamilton, Edith, *The Greek Way*. New York: Norton, 1930.

Hawkins, Gerald, *Stonehenge Decoded*. New York: Doubleday, 1965.

Hibbert, Christopher, *The Search for King Arthur*. New York: Harper & Row, 1969.

Herrmann, Paul, *Conquest by Man*. New York: Harper & Row, 1954.

Ivimy, John, *The Sphinx and the Megaliths*. New York: Harper & Row, 1975.

Josephy, Alvin M. (editor), *History of Africa*. New York: American Heritage, 1971.

Keller, Werner, *The Bible as History*, translated by William Neil. New York: Morrow, 1956.

——, *The Etruscans*, translated by William Neil. New York: Knopf, 1974.

Kenyon, Kathleen M., *Digging Up Jericho*. London: Ernest Benn, 1957.

Kramer, Samuel Noah, *Cradle of Civilization*. New York: Time-Life Books, 1967.

*Last Two Million Years, The*. London: Reader's Digest Assn., 1973.

Lawrence, D. H., *Etruscan Places*. New York: Viking, 1932.

Marinatos, Spyridon, "Thera, Key to the Riddle of Minos," *National Geographic*, May 1972.

Marshall, John, *Mohenjo-Daro and the Indus Civilization*. London: Arthur Probsthain, 1931.

McKendrick, Melveena, *Spain*. New York: American Heritage, 1972.

Morris, Jan, "The Best-Traveled Man on Earth," *Horizon*, Summer 1975.

Mumford, Lewis, *Technics and Civilization*. New York: Harcourt, Brace, 1934.

——, "The First Megamachine," *Daedalus*, Spring 1965.

Pallottino, Massimo, *The Etruscans*. Bloomington: Indiana University Press, 1975.

Pendlebury, J. D. S., *The Archaeology of Crete*. London: Methuen, 1939.

Schliemann, Heinrich, *Ilios*. London: John Murray, 1880.

Stanford, W. B., *The Quest for Ulysses*. New York: Praeger, 1974.

Thom, Alexander, *Megalithic Sites in Britain*. London: Faber & Faber, 1959.

van der Post, Laurens, "Portrait of a Continent," in *The World of Mankind*. New York: Golden Press, 1962.

Vansina, Jan, "Inner Africa," in *History of Africa*. New York: American Heritage, 1971.

Wellard, James, *The Search for the Etruscans*. New York: Saturday Review, 1973.

Wells, H. G., *Outline of History*. New York: Macmillan, 1924.

Wheeler, Sir Mortimer, *The Indus Civilization*. Cambridge: Cambridge University Press, 1953.

——, *Aspects of the Ascent of a Civilization*. London: Oxford University Press, 1955.

White, R. J., *England*. New York: McGraw-Hill, 1971.

Woolley, Sir Leonard, *Excavations at Ur*. London: Ernest Benn, 1954.

Wright, G. Ernest, *Great People of the Bible*. New York: Reader's Digest Assn., 1974.

## ABOUT THE AUTHOR

ALAN LANDSBURG is a successful film and television producer, heading up his own production company in Los Angeles, California. He was instrumental in bringing the von Däniken phenomenon to the attention of the American public through TV by producing "In Search of Ancient Astronauts." Alan Landsburg is also the author of *In Search of Ancient Mysteries* and *The Outer Space Connection.* He is currently working on a weekly television series, "In Search Of . . . ," which has been on the air since September, 1976. *In Search of Lost Civilizations* and five future books on magic and witchcraft, extraterrestrials, monsters, special phenomena and people, are based on this series.